"Bolz-Weber is a surprisingly vulnerable narrator who pairs personal confessions with beautifully articulated statements of faith."
—THE CHRISTIAN CENTURY

"Engaging and accessible...Bolz-Weber is clear-eyed about the personal travails faced by the marginalized and those without faith."
—BOOKLIST

"This is an astonishing book...contagious, honest, captivating...a rare gift...I realize that I'm gushing, but that's what you do when a book inspires and moves and touches you like this one does."
—ROB BELL, author of *What We Talk About When We Talk About God* and *Love Wins*

"For anyone who is Christian, interested in Christianity, anti-Christian (or anti-Religion), I recommend this book."
—GORDON GANO, lead singer, Violent Femmes

"Pastor Nadia Bolz-Weber speaks the truth of our humanity that we too often want to deny. She declares the radical power of God's grace for Jesus's sake that we so often water down rather than daily be drowned in it. Yes, read at your own risk."
—FORMER PRESIDING BISHOP MARK HANSON, Evangelical Lutheran Church in America (ELCA)

"Funny, raw, and packed with truth, this book is offensive in all the right ways...This book reminded me of why I am a Christian, and I wept with gratitude when I finished it."
—RACHEL HELD EVANS, blogger, author of *A Year of Biblical Womanhood*

"Nadia has written a wonderful, rule-breaking, stereotype-smashing book that succeeds as a memoir, as a sermon on love, and as a welcome home 'letter' to the rejected. With this book, Nadia will become America's pastor to those alienated from religion but who still crave transcendent purpose."
—FRANK SCHAEFFER, author of *Crazy for God*

ACCIDENTAL SAINtS

ALSO BY NADIA BOLZ-WEBER:

Pastrix: The Cranky, Beautiful Faith of a Sinner & Saint

Salvation on the Small Screen

NADIA BOLZ-WEBER

ACCIDENTAL

SAINTS

FINDING GOD IN ALL
THE WRONG PEOPLE

CONVERGENT
BOOKS

ACCIDENTAL SAINTS
PUBLISHED BY CONVERGENT BOOKS

All Scripture quotations are taken from the New Revised Standard Version of the Bible, copyright © 1989 by the Division of Christian Education of the National Council of the Churches of Christ in the USA. Used by permission. All rights reserved.

Details in some anecdotes and stories have been changed to protect the identities of the persons involved.

Hardcover ISBN 978-160142-755-7
eBook ISBN 978-160142-757-1

Cover design by Jessie Sayward Bright; cover image of Bertie the Tattooed Lady tattooed by Charles "Red" Gibbons, c.1920 (black-and-white photo), American School (twentieth century)/ Private Collection/Prismatic Pictures/Bridgeman Images

Published in the United States by Convergent Books, an imprint of the Crown Publishing Group, a division of Penguin Random House LLC, New York.

CONVERGENT BOOKS® and its open book colophon are registered trademarks of Penguin Random House LLC.

Library of Congress Cataloging-in-Publication Data
Bolz-Weber, Nadia.
    Accidental saints : finding God in all the wrong people / Nadia Bolz-Weber—First Edition.
        pages cm
    ISBN 978-1-60142-755-7—ISBN 978-1-60142-757-1 (electronic) 1. House for All Sinners and Saints (Denver, Colo.)—Biography. 2. Christian biography. I. Title.
    BX8076.D46B65 2015
    284.1'78883—dc23   277.3093
                        No 9 (Bolz-Webr 2015012506

Printed in the United States of America
2015—First Edition

10 9 8 7 6 5 4 3 2 1

✤

For the people of House for All Sinners and Saints.
You make me believe.

Contents

1 Saint Cookies 3

2 Absolution for Assholes 13

3 My Lowest for His Highest 21

4 Whale Spit in the Superdome 31

5 You Are Not "The Blessing" 41

6 A Thief in the Night 53

7 Mary, Mother of Our Lord 63

8 The Slaughter of the Holy Innocents of
Sandy Hook Elementary 71

9 Frances 83

10 Panic Attack in Jericho 93

11 Parlors 105

12 The Lame 115

13 Dirty Feet 129

14 The Dogs of Good Friday 137

15 Vignettes from an Easter Vigil 145

16 Charcoal Fires and Jail Cells 155

17 Judas Will Now Take Your Confession 163

18 The Best Shitty Feeling in the World 173

19 Blessed Are They 181

A Note to Readers 193

Acknowledgments 195

Discussion Questions 197

A Conversation with the Author 203

Rejoice, now, all heavenly powers! Sing, choirs of angels! Exult, all creation around God's throne! Jesus Christ is risen!

Celebrate the divine mysteries with exultation; and for so great a victory, sound the trumpet of salvation.

Rejoice, O earth, in shining splendor, radiant in the brightness of your king!

Christ has conquered! Glory fills you!

Darkness vanishes forever.

Rejoice, O holy church! Exult in glory!

The risen Savior shines upon you!

Let this place resound with joy, echoing the mighty song of all God's people.[1]

---

1. These readings are taken from the "Exsultet," an ancient Christian hymn that is sung as part of the Easter Vigil.

1

---
†

Saint Cookies

E arly in the life of House for All Sinners and Saints, we began a
tradition of making "saint cookies" on All Saints' Sunday.[2]

I had scoured the Internet for old or weird practices we could
borrow, and I am certain I read something that described how, in
Finland or someplace like that, people make saint cookies, little gingerbread men and women who get handed out as part of the All Saints'
Sunday celebration. I swear that's what I remember.

So when we were baking up our church from scratch, a few folks
gathered in my kitchen to bake up some gingerbread men and women
from scratch, thinking it was a thing.

At one point, I realized that what our little brown saint cookies
really needed were halos, obviously, so we painted shiny yellow glaze
around the top of each round-headed gingerbread man and woman
(which made them look not so much holy as blond).

"How about these?" Victoria asked when she arrived, holding up

---

2. The November 1 feast day when the church recognizes how thin the veil is between life and
death and remembers that the church includes all who have gone before us and now are
glorified and all who will follow, who are yet to be born. We ring a bell for each loved one
who has died since the last All Saints' Sunday, and we, the saints who are still on earth,
honor all of those, also called saints, who have passed from this life and into the one to come.

two extralarge cookie cutters. She's always been slightly mischievous for a social worker. I think it's the red hair. "The cookies for my saints need to be special," she offered. Before the evening was over, Victoria was proudly showing off two special saint cookies that stood inches above their fellows. One, a woman, had flames of red and yellow licking her skirt, accompanied by big eyes and an open mouth that looked borrowed from Mr. Bill.

"Um, Joan of Arc?" I guessed correctly. Next to Joan was a fellow saint, but this one looked like he was wearing a belted one-shoulder caveman outfit and he was missing his head. "Martyred Fred Flintstone?" I guessed incorrectly.

"John the Baptist," she said proudly. Of course. Victoria volunteered to bring the basket of completed saint cookies to hand out after liturgy the next day. Not surprisingly, they proved to be a great way to bring some levity to what was to be an otherwise heavy liturgy.

What we now know is that saint cookies are not a tradition anywhere but House for All Sinners and Saints—at least nowhere I could find when I went back to the Internet later. Apparently, I just dreamed that shit up.

Victoria's basket of saint cookies sat on the edge of a long series of draped white tables that lined the wall. Each table was dotted with candles, marigolds, and various remembrances of the dead: The worn soft denim overalls of someone's granddaddy who was a farmer. An icon of Mary Magdalene. An icon of Cesar Chavez. A photo of a group of friends from the '80s. A child's blanket. A shrine that my parishioner Amy Clifford had made for Vincent van Gogh—a small painted box that stood on end, his self-portrait glued to the inside, and ears, one of which was missing a piece, glued to the sides.

Apart from those who have fallen in combat, Americans tend to forget our ancestors, and we spend as little time as possible publicly mourning them. But in the church, we do the very odd thing of proclaiming that the dead are still a part of us, a part of our lives, and are even an animating presence in the church. Saint Paul describes the saints as "a great cloud of witnesses," so when they have passed, we still hold them up, hoping perhaps that their virtues—their ability to have faith in God in the face of an oppressive empire or a failing crop or the blight of cancer—might become our own virtue, our own strength.

As I surveyed the basket of saint cookies sitting next to the lovingly arranged photos, shrines, and names simply written on index cards, I was thinking how amazing it is that there's a holy day when we honor those who have gone before. And then I saw *her* name. I winced, even though I was the one who had hesitantly written it: Alma White.

A couple of months earlier, I had been walking down Sherman Street in Denver with my parishioner Amy Clifford, an artsy, thoughtful, passionate woman who had been by my side, helping to build our church. On our walk that day, we noticed a sizable memorial of sorts in the courtyard of a large, weird-looking church across the street from the Colorado capitol building.

The roof of the Pillar of Fire Church is crowned with the enormous pink call letters KPOF that light up at night, making it look like what it is: a Pentecostal church that doubles as a radio station.

We squinted to read the inscription on the memorial: "Alma White, founder of the Pillar of Fire Church, 1901." Turning to Amy I said, "Alma? That's a woman's name, isn't it? Did a *woman* plant a church in Denver in 1901?"

I didn't know of many women who had set out to start churches all by themselves, much less at the turn of the twentieth century, so, desperate as I was for someone I could place in the category "hero" and "role model" (since I, too, was setting out to be a female pastor of a new church in Denver), I pulled out my phone and Googled Alma White. My excitement about discovering a hero only built as I read her Wikipedia entry: "Alma Bridwell White (June 16, 1862–June 26, 1946) was the founder and a bishop of the Pillar of Fire Church." *[Oh my gosh. It's true!]* I went on to read that in 1918, she became the first female bishop in the United States. She was noted for her feminism *[Yes!]* and her association with *[wait for it . . .]* the Ku Klux Klan, her anti-Catholicism, anti-Semitism, anti-Pentecostalism, racism, and hostility to immigrants. *[Fuck.]*

The next day I called my Episcopal friend Sara to tell her the story of how I thought I had a hero only to find out she was just a lousy racist. Sara's response? "E-mail me her name. I'll add her to the Litany of Saints along with all the other broken people of God."

I didn't want Alma White's name on the Litany of Saints. Having her name lying on the table, illuminated by the nearby paschal candle,[3] alongside the names of Saint Francis and Cesar Chavez, felt wrong. I want racists to stay in the "racist" box. When they start sneaking into the "saint" box, it makes me nervous. But that's how it works. On All Saints' Sunday, I am faced with sticky ambiguities around saints who were bad and sinners who were good.

Personally, I think knowing the difference between a racist and a saint is kind of important. But when Jesus again and again says things like the last shall be first, and the first shall be last, and the poor are blessed, and the rich are cursed, and that prostitutes make great dinner guests, it makes me wonder if our need for pure black-and-white

---

3. A paschal candle is a large candle that represents the light of Christ in the world; it's traditionally initiated at the Easter Vigil and then displayed during special occasions throughout the year.

categories is not true religion but maybe actually a sin. Knowing what category to place hemlock in might help us know whether it's safe to drink, but knowing what category to place ourselves and others in does not help us know God in the way that the church so often has tried to convince us it does.

And anyway, it has been my experience that what makes us the saints of God is not our ability to be saintly but rather God's ability to work through sinners. The title "saint" is always conferred, never earned. Or as the good Saint Paul puts it, "For it is God who is at work in you, enabling you both to will and to work for his good pleasure" (Philippians 2:13). I have come to realize that *all* the saints I've known have been accidental ones—people who inadvertently stumbled into redemption like they were looking for something else at the time, people who have just a wee bit of a drinking problem and manage to get sober and help others to do the same, people who are as kind as they are hostile.

Next to Alma on our All Saints' table was an icon of another accidental saint, Harvey Milk (the first openly gay person elected to public office in California, who was shot to death by a fellow city employee in 1978). The icon showed Milk standing in front of the Golden Gate Bridge with five silver bullet holes in his chest and a golden halo behind his head. The icon was created by Bill, one of our congregation's artists, who called me later when someone challenged him for creating a visual representation of sainthood for someone who was not Christian.

I explained to Bill that what we celebrate in the saints is not their piety or perfection but the fact that we believe in a God who gets redemptive and holy things done in this world through, of all things, human beings, all of whom are flawed.

I really do believe that. And yet, when I hung up the phone, all I could think about was how hard it is for me to believe that what's true of Alma White or Harvey Milk might also be true for me—that maybe God can use me despite the fact that I, in so many ways, am ill-suited for the work I do.

Yet that is my experience. I keep making mistakes, even the same ones over and over. I repeatedly attempt (and fail) to keep God and my fellow humans at arm's length. I say no when I should say yes. I say yes when I should say no. I stumble into holy moments not realizing where I am until they are over. I love poorly, then accidently say the right thing at the right moment without even realizing it, then forget what matters, then show tenderness when it's needed, and then turn around and think of myself way too often.

I simply continue to be a person on whom God is at work. And I don't even seek that out, to be honest. I admire those who take on "spiritual practices," who seek a sense of well-being through yoga or meditation or quiet times, but other than lifting really heavy weights every morning at my CrossFit gym, I honestly can't think of what practices I do that help me become more spiritual. I *can,* however, talk endlessly about the way I've been thrown on my ass over and over by the Bible, the practices of the church, and the people of God. That is to say, by religion.

I recently was asked by an earnest young seminarian during a Q&A, "Pastor Nadia, what do you do personally to get closer to God?"

Before I even realized I was saying it, I replied, "What? Nothing. Sounds like a horrible idea to me, trying to get *closer* to God." Half the time, I wish God would leave me alone. Getting closer to God might mean getting told to love someone I don't even like, or to give away even more of my money. It might mean letting some idea or dream that is dear to me get ripped away.

My spirituality is most active, not in meditation, but in the moments when:

I realize God may have gotten something beautiful done through me despite the fact that I am an asshole,

and when I am confronted by the mercy of the gospel so much that I cannot hate my enemies,

and when I am unable to judge the sin of someone else (which, let's be honest, I *love* to do) because my own crap is too much in the way,

and when I have to bear witness to another human being's suffering despite my desire to be left alone,

and when I am forgiven by someone even though I don't deserve it and my forgiver does this because he, too, is trapped by the gospel,

and when traumatic things happen in the world and I have nowhere to place them or make sense of them but what I *do* have is a group of people who gather with me every week, people who will mourn and pray with me over the devastation of something like a school shooting,

and when I end up changed by loving someone I'd never choose out of a catalog but whom God sends my way to teach me about God's love.

But none of these things are a result of spiritual practices or disciplines, as admirable as those things can be. They are born in a religious life, in a life bound by ritual and community, by repetition, by work, by giving and receiving, by mandated grace.

This is the form church takes at House for All. As Stephen, one of my parishioners, puts it, "Our 'ministry' is Word and Sacrament—everything else flows from that. We see a need, we fill it. We fuck up, we say sorry. We ask for grace and prayers when we need them (a lot). Jesus shows up for us through each other. We eat, we pray, we sing, we fall, we get up, repeat. Not that complicated."

There are many reasons to steer clear of Christianity. No question. I fully understand why people make that choice. Christianity has survived some unspeakable abominations: the Crusades, clergy sex-scandals, papal corruption, televangelist scams, and clown ministry. But it will survive us, too. It will survive our mistakes and pride and exclusion of others. I believe that the power of Christianity—the thing that made the very first disciples drop their nets and walk away from everything they knew, the thing that caused Mary Magdalene to return to the tomb and then announce the resurrection of Christ, the thing that the early Christians martyred themselves for, and the thing that keeps me in the Jesus business (or, what my Episcopal priest friend Paul calls "working for the company")—is something that cannot be killed. The power of unbounded mercy, of what we call The Gospel, cannot be destroyed by corruption and toothy TV preachers. Because in the end, there is still Jesus.

And I can't shake Jesus, though I've tried. The gospel, this story of a God who came to us through Jesus and who loved without bounds and forgave without reservation and said that we have the power to do the same, cannot be destroyed by all the stupid mistakes you will read about in the chapters that follow. These mistakes, sins, and failings are mine, but perhaps they are also *ours*. And the redemption is ours, too. Because if Alma White cannot destroy the Light that shines in all her darkness, maybe we can't either.

On that All Saints' table, between the basket of saint cookies and the card showing Alma White's name, we set our first paschal candle, recently purchased at the Catholic bookstore. During the Easter Vigil and throughout the coming year, we would use it to symbolize Christ's presence in our midst.

That year, the candle was new and white. But each paschal candle since then has been created by Victoria out of the melted down remains of all the candles used in the previous months of liturgies, so that, like our church itself, the candle in our midst has a lot of beautiful imperfections in it. The beeswax is smooth and golden but flecked with bits of burned wick and debris. Like the burned-down remains of our own stories that we carry with us, and like the imperfect bits of our humanity that bring texture to the divine love we also carry.

We melt and are formed into something new, but the burned bits remain.

2

Absolution for Assholes

I had already finished my Americano by the time Larry showed up for our coffee date. He was a few minutes late, which was no big deal, but this meant that when we sat down on the leather sofa on the bottom floor of my favorite Denver coffee house, I didn't have a drink to distract me from the conversation I had been dreading.

"This is cool!" he said, looking around at the bordello-meets-library look of the place. "It just took me longer to get here than I expected. But I'm glad to be here because I've just been *so excited* that I get to have coffee with you!"

"Me too!" I lied.

I wasn't excited. I was uncomfortable. Larry had cornered me the Sunday before, his first time visiting the church. He had grabbed my arm, his glassy eyes looking for an uncomfortably long time into mine, and began talking about how much he loved my sermon at Red Rocks[4] and how excited he was to learn that he could even come to my church.

He then talked a lot about FDR and the Democratic Party—two

---

4. Red Rocks is a natural amphitheater in the foothills outside of Denver and is the location of a city-wide sunrise Easter service. About ten thousand people attend each year.

of his passions. I don't remember much else from that coffee date, except that I had no idea what to say.

I *never* knew what to say to Larry. It felt like he was at church because he thought he could connect with me, not because he was hoping to connect with God and other people, and while I may very well have been wrong about his motivations, that kind of thing makes me uncomfortable whether it's real or not. Plus, I just didn't like him. And not even for any interesting reasons, just age, gender, zip code, breath, waistband. You know, the shit horrible people judge regular nice people for because we are miserable bastards. So I kept Larry at arm's length, never doing much to try to connect with him, never bothering to help get him connected. And soon it would be too late.

✢

"Hello?" Caitlin answered her phone. Thank God.

"Can you meet me for confession and absolution? Like, now?" I wished I had one of those old phone cords so I could twist it around my hand. Sometimes a good fidget can transfer the shakiness from your voice to your fingers.

Caitlin and I met in seminary. She, too, was raised in the Church of Christ and discovered Lutheranism later in life on her way to becoming a pastor. That's pretty much where the similarities end. Years ago when we were both planning our fortieth birthday parties—mine a roller disco party at a rink I rented out, and hers with a group of close friends watching the sunrise on a hill overlooking the city—I commented that the difference between our two birthday celebrations illuminates the difference between our two personalities. She has so many lovely personality traits that I just don't possess. Caitlin replied, "Of course you do, Nadia, they just aren't your favorite ones."

This kind of thing is why Caitlin is my "mother confessor." She knows me. Really well. And she is unimpressed with my sin. I've told her things about myself that I've not told anyone else and she still wants to be my friend. Not because she is magnanimous but because she believes in the power of forgiveness and the grace of God. You'd think this would be true of all clergy, but trust me when I tell you it's not.

"A parishioner of mine died today," I told her, "and I can't go comfort his wife until I confess something awful."

"Come on over," she said.

An hour later, as I walked into her office, she joked, "Wait. You didn't *kill* him, did you?"

Nope. I hadn't killed Larry. I just hadn't been a very good pastor to the guy, even though, unlike myself, he was really nice. And now he was dead and I had to comfort his widow and I knew I couldn't be present to her grief if all I could think of was that stupid thing I did to him recently, which wasn't very nice.

It was a thing no one would ever know I'd done but that I simply had to confess and be absolved of: I'd purposely left Larry's address off a mass e-mail I sent out, reminding people to register for the spring retreat. Seriously. Who does a thing like that? It had weighed on me ever since, even though in the grand scheme of crime and betrayal it was, at worst, a misdemeanor.

There's the horrible feeling you get when someone you love has been diagnosed with a brain tumor and then there's the horrible feeling you get when someone you've thought bad things about, someone who is actually a really great guy (though you are an asshole and tried to make sure he wasn't going to bring his too-baggy pants and his halitosis to the church retreat), has been diagnosed with a brain tumor. It was something that weighed on my conscience, something I would be ashamed of if anyone else knew. Actually I was plenty ashamed just being the only one who knew. But we all hide things for ourselves—that time we spanked our child too hard, the times we have to erase our browser history, the time we lied about ourselves to get a job, the times we flirt online with people who aren't our spouses. Whatever it is, we all carry secrets. As the old chain-smoking guys in my twelve-step program say, "You're only as sick as your secrets, kid." So I had to tell Caitlin my sin against Larry before I could, with a clean conscience, go comfort his new wife.

Okay, fine, so there was one other thing I'd done to Larry. Hardly worth mentioning . . .

A week after Larry was diagnosed with a brain tumor, he had e-mailed me saying that he and his girlfriend were afraid of him dying and they wanted to get married the following week, and would I do the wedding? Fortunately, I had an out. As I explained to Caitlin in her office, my policy has always been to undergo a series of premarital counseling sessions before officiating anyone's wedding, so I said I'm sorry, but I couldn't. In the end they got a shaman who was a friend of his fiancée to officiate.

But the fact is, if my longtime parishioners Jim and Stuart, or another couple I love, had become deathly ill and wanted to get married right away, I'd have done it in a heartbeat. I just didn't want to do *this* wedding. So I gave them the excuse about premarital counseling and even got my bishop to cosign. (I e-mailed asking if he thought a medical shot-gun wedding was something I should do and he said probably not.)

Caitlin kindly listened. I plunged ahead.

Of course, taking cover behind a more "legitimate" excuse than "I don't feel like it" isn't exactly a lie, I admitted, but it doesn't erase the truth. It's a common thing people do. We make lame excuses to get out of commitments, or we blame other people for the fact that we can't show up. But sometimes we create these smoke screens to divert attention from the truth of our own decisions and shortcomings. Often we even fool ourselves with these excuses, but there are times when the truth won't let us go. Sure, I can avoid other people's scrutiny by telling my bullshit side of the story over and over to anyone who will listen. But I know the truth. And sometimes it all catches up with me at night as I lie in bed—in that not-quite-awake and not-quite-asleep place. In those moments, my ego is turned off, perhaps for the only time all day. In that consciousness-minus-ego state, the truth fights past the layers of food and entertainment and all the other distractions I shovel on top of it and, unbidden, crawls its way back up into my thoughts.

"Does everyone have these moments?" I wondered aloud to Caitlin. Perhaps some feel their errors in life aren't bad enough to fret over, or perhaps they've built enough protective layers around their ego that they have successfully avoided feeling shamed by their secrets altogether. But like Matt Damon's character in the film *Good Will Hunting*, if they were confronted with limitless and repetitive grace, like that offered by the counselor Robin Williams played, they'd eventually crack. Not because they should, but because we all do. Right? Because we are all burdened by the ugly things we've done and continue to do.

And for me, as much insulation as my ego provides during my waking hours, it clocks out as I'm about to fall asleep, and it's then that the uglier truths claw their way to the surface. Oddly, it's in these times that I feel closest to God. Not when I'm on a mountaintop, but when I'm lying in bed half-asleep, feeling defenseless.

But as soon as my ego reengages, it's game over. I can take it from here.

Thinking back, I can say that maybe my sin toward Larry doesn't rank up there with embezzling tithes or schtupping the choir director, but if someone comes to your church and you make up excuses to not serve them with grace and love, it's still despicable. And the fact that I "learned" from it all and haven't done that kind of thing since doesn't make up for it, because I'm sure if I had a minute, I could come up with other things I've done in its stead. Which means that I am in perpetual need of grace.

Quietly, Caitlin took it all in. She took a drink of her water, then reached out for my hand and said, "Nadia, Jesus died for our sins. Including that one."

Including that one. Including every one.

It feels like a strange and abstract thing to say. "Jesus died for your sins." And I've squandered plenty of ink arguing against the notion that God had to kill Jesus because we were bad. But when Caitlin said that Jesus died for our sins, including that one, I was reminded again that there is nothing we have done that God cannot redeem. Small betrayals, large infractions, minor offenses. All of it.

Some would say that instead of the cross being about Jesus standing in for us to take the really bad spanking from God for our own naughtiness (the fancy theological term for this is substitutionary atonement), what happens at the cross is a "blessed exchange." God gathers up all our sin, all our broken-ass junk, into God's own self and transforms all that death into life. Jesus takes our crap and exchanges it for his blessedness.

The blessed exchange (and not substitutionary atonement) always just made so much more sense to me as an idea. But sometimes ideas become reality, like when a blessed exchange happened in Larry's backyard after I gave a short homily at his memorial service.

✢

I wish I could say that, after the absolution Caitlin proclaimed to me, I was totally freed from any burden of conscience, but that's not entirely true. It didn't totally happen until a middle-aged white lady came up to me and said, "You're Nadia, right?"

She took my hands and looked startlingly straight into my eyes. "I wanted to thank you for having a church where Larry felt so welcome. He spoke so highly of you and your congregation, and I know that having you as his pastor meant a lot for him in his final months."

There it was. A blessed exchange. My crap for Jesus's mercy.

I will never know Larry. I'll never know what it is like to love him, to see him, to know what the source of his tenderness toward his wife was or from where he drew his strength in his final days. That is all lost to me. But for some reason our congregation was a place of comfort for him.

Sometimes God needs some stuff done, even though I can be a real asshole. There is absolutely no justice in the fact that Larry loved me and that church. But if I got what I deserved in this life, I'd be screwed—so instead, I receive that grace for what it is: a gift.

3

·❖·

My Lowest for His Highest

W ell, *friend,* want to go to the shooting range with me?" Clayton said, his light brown eyes lighting up mischievously. We were stretching before the CrossFit class Clayton coaches when I mentioned that I'd recently realized he was my "token conservative friend," the way some people have a "token black friend." His response was to invite me to, of all things, a gun range.

I reached for my toes as my liberal gun-control-advocate self immediately and gleefully replied, "Seriously? Of course I do." Because politics should never, if at all possible, get in the way of fun.

Little did I know that this would be one of several experiences, during what turned out to be the week of the George Zimmerman acquittal, that would make it virtually impossible for me to claim the liberal outrage/moral high ground I would later wish I could maintain, since life and its ambiguities sometimes throw our ideals into crisis.

·❖·

A few days after his offer, I saw Clayton's short, muscular frame walking up to my front door carrying a heavy black bag. He was there for a quick gun-safety lesson before we headed to the range, since I had never in my life actually held a handgun. Clayton is a Texan, a Republican, and a Second Amendment enthusiast. But since Clayton has a degree from Texas A&M and has lived part of his life in Saudi Arabia, where his dad was an oil man, he describes himself as a "well-educated and well-traveled redneck."

"There are four things you need to know," Clayton said, beginning my very first gun-safety lesson. "One, always assume every gun you pick up is loaded. Two, never aim a gun at something you do not intend to destroy. Three, keep your finger off the trigger until you are ready to fire, and four, know your target and what's beyond it. A gun is basically a paperweight. In and of themselves," he claimed, "they are only dangerous if people do not follow these rules."

I'm not sure what the statistics are on gun-shaped paperweight deaths, I thought, *but I'll be sure to look that up.*

"Okay, ready?" Clayton asked.

"I have no idea," I replied.

He placed a matte black handgun and a box of ammunition on our kitchen table, and it felt as illicit as if he had just placed a kilo of cocaine or a stack of *Hustler* magazines on the very surface where we pray and eat our dinners as a family.

I tried to ask some intelligent questions. "What kind of gun is this?"

"It's a 40." Like I had any idea what the hell that meant.

"What's a 9mm? I've heard a lot about those."

"This is." And he lifted his shirt up to show his concealed handgun.

"Man, you don't carry that thing around all the time, do you?"

He smiled. "If I'm not in gym shorts or pajamas, yes."

Later, in the firing-range parking lot, filled almost exclusively with pickup trucks, I made the astute observation, "No Obama bumper stickers."

"Weird, huh?" he joked.

When I'm someplace cool, say an old cathedral or a hipster ice cream shop, I am sure to check in on Facebook. But not here. Partly because it was Monday morning and Clayton had penciled in our fun shooting date as a "work meeting," but also because I didn't want a rash of shit from my friends or parishioners—almost all of whom are liberal—asking if I'd lost my mind or simply been abducted by rednecks.

As we stepped onto the casing-littered, black rubber-matted floor of the indoor firing range, I was aware of several important points: one, our guns were loaded and intended to destroy the paper target in front of us; two, I should put my finger on the trigger only when I intended to shoot; three, a wall of rubber and concrete was behind my target; and four, I sweat.

I knew from hearing gunshots in my neighborhood that guns were loud. And I knew from the movies that there was a kickback when a gun was fired. But, holy shit, was I unprepared for how loud and jolting firing a handgun would be. Or how fun.

We shot for about an hour, and after we were done, Clayton told me that I did pretty well, for a first-timer. (Except for when a hot shell casing went down my shirt and I jerked around so mindlessly that he had to reach over and turn the loaded gun in my hand back toward the target, making me feel like a total dumbass. A really, really dangerous dumbass.)

But I loved it. I loved it like I love roller coasters and riding a motorcycle: not something I want in my life all the time, but an activity that is fun to do once in a while, that makes me feel like I'm alive and a little bit lethal.

"Can we shoot skeet next time?" I asked eagerly as we made our way back to the camo-covered front desk to retrieve our IDs. The whole shop looked like a duck blind. As though if something dangerous or tasty came through the front door, all the young, acne-ridden guys who work there could take it down without danger of being spotted.

On the way back to my house, I suggested we stop for pupusas (stuffed Salvadorian corn cakes) so that we both could have a novel experience on a Monday.

Sitting at one of the five stools by the window at Tacos Acapulco— looking out on the check-cashing joints and Mexican panaderias that dot East Colfax Avenue—I took the opportunity to ask a burning question: "So why in the world do you want to carry a gun all the time?" I'd never knowingly been this close to a gun-carrier before, and it felt like my chance to ask something I'd always wanted to know. I could only hope my question didn't feel to him like it does to our black friend Shayla when people ask to touch her afro.

As he tried managing with his fork the melted cheese that refused to detach itself from the pupusa, he said, "Self-defense, and pride of country. We have this right, so we should exercise it. Also if someone tried to hurt us while we were sitting here, I could take them down."

It was a foreign worldview to me, that people could go through life so aware of the possibility that someone might try to hurt them, and that, as a response, they would strap a gun on their body as they made their way through Denver. I didn't understand or even approve. But Clayton is my token conservative friend, and I love him, and he went through the trouble of taking me to the shooting range, so I left it there.

✢

The week I went shooting with Clayton was also the week of my mother's seventieth and my sister's fiftieth birthday party. It was a murder mystery dinner, so, five nights after blasting paper targets with Clayton at the shooting range, I sat on the back patio of my parents' suburban Denver home and pretended to be a hippie winemaker for the sake of a contrived drama. Normally, my natural misanthropy would prevent me from participating in such awkward nonsense, but I soon remembered how many times I had voluntarily dressed myself up and played a role in other contrived dramas that didn't involve a four-course meal or civil company (like the year I tried to be a Deadhead), so I submitted to the murder mystery dinner for the sake of two women I love. My role called for a flowing skirt, peasant blouse, and flowers in my hair—none of which I own or could possibly endure wearing, so a nightgown and lots of beads had to do the trick.

Throughout the mostly pleasant evening, I would see Mom talking to my brother out of the side of her mouth, just like she did when we were kids and she wanted to tell Dad something she didn't want us to know. I watched my mom, unaware that an unscripted drama was unfolding around the edges of the fictional one that called for flowers in my fauxhawk.

As I snuck into the kitchen to check my phone for messages, my dad followed me to fill me in on what was happening. It turns out my mom's side-of-the-mouth whispers were about something serious. My mom had been receiving threats from an unbalanced (and reportedly armed) woman who was blaming my mom for a loss she had experienced. My mom had nothing to do with this loss, but that didn't stop this woman from fixating on her as the one to blame. And she knew where my mom went to church on Sundays.

"It's made being at church pretty tense for us," my father told me.

My older brother Gary, who is a law enforcement officer in a federal prison and who, along with his wife and three kids, attends the same church as my parents, walked by Dad and me in the kitchen and said, "Horrible, right? The past three weeks I've carried a concealed weapon to church in case she shows up and tries anything."

I immediately thought of Clayton and his heretofore foreign worldview, weighing it against how I now felt instinctually glad that my brother would be able to react if a crazy person tried to hurt our mother. And how, at the same time, it felt like madness that I would be glad someone was carrying a gun to church. But that's the thing about my values—they tend to bump up against reality, and when that happens, I may need to throw them out the window. That, or I ignore reality. For me, more often than not, it's the values that go.

My gut reaction to my brother's gun-carrying disturbed me, but not as much in the moment as it would the next morning.

✝

On the night of the party, I missed the breaking news that George Zimmerman, who had shot and killed unarmed teen Trayvon Martin, had been found not guilty on all counts. For more than a year, the case had ignited fierce debate over racism and Florida's "Stand Your Ground" law, which allows the use of violent force if someone believes their life is being threatened.

My Facebook feed was lit up with protests, outrage, and rants. I wanted to join in and act as a voice for nonviolence that week, but when I heard on NPR that George Zimmerman's brother was saying he rejected the idea that Trayvon Martin was unarmed, Martin's weapon being the sidewalk on which he broke George's nose, well, my first reaction was not nonviolence but an overwhelming urge to reach through the radio and give that man a fully armed punch in the throat.

Even more, that very week, a federal law enforcement officer was carrying a concealed weapon into my mom's church every Sunday. Which is insane and something I would normally want to post a rant about on my Facebook wall for all the liberals like me to "like." Except in this case, that particular law enforcement officer (a) was my brother, and (b) carried that weapon to protect his (my) family, his (my) mother, from a crazy woman who wanted her dead. When I heard that my brother was armed to protect my own mom, I wasn't alarmed like any good gun-control supporting pastor would be. I was relieved. And now what the hell do I post on Facebook? What do I do with that?

I also had to deal with the fact that I simply could not express the level of antiracist outrage I wanted to, knowing something that no one else would know unless I said it out loud: despite my politics and liberalism, when a group of young black men in my neighborhood walk by, my gut reaction is to brace myself in a different way than I would if those men were white. I hate this about myself, but if I said that there is not residual racism in me, racism that—after forty-four years of being reinforced by messages in the media and culture around me—I simply do not know how to escape, I would be lying. Even if I do own an "eracism" bumper sticker.

The morning after the George Zimmerman verdict, as I was reflecting on what to say to my church about it, I wanted to be a voice for nonviolence, antiracism, and gun-control as I felt I should (or as I saw people on Twitter demanding: "If your pastor doesn't preach about gun control and racism this week, find a new church")—but all I could do was stand in my kitchen and cry. Cry for all my inconsistencies. For my parishioner and mother of two, Andrea Gutierrez, who said to me that mothers of kids with brown and black skin now feel like their children can legally be target practice on the streets of suburbia. For a nation divided—both sides hating the other. For all the ways I silently perpetuate the things I criticize. For the death threats toward my family and the death threats toward the Zimmerman family. For Tracy Martin and Sybrina Fulton, whose child, Trayvon, was shot dead, and who were told that it was more his fault than the fault of the shooter.

Moments after hearing about the acquittal, I walked my dog and called Duffy, a particularly thoughtful parishioner. "I'm really screwed up about all of this," I said, proceeding to detail all the reasons that, even though I feel so strongly about these issues, I could not with any integrity "stand my own ground" against violence and racism—not because I no longer believe in standing against those things (I do), but because my own life and my own heart contain too much ambiguity. There is both violence and nonviolence in me, and yet I don't *believe* in them both. She suggested that maybe others felt the same way and that maybe what they needed from their pastor wasn't the moral outrage and rants they were already seeing on Facebook; maybe they just needed me to confess my own crippling inconsistencies as a way for them to acknowledge their own.

That felt like a horrible idea, but I knew she was right.

So often in the church, being a pastor or a "spiritual leader" means being the example of "godly living." A pastor is supposed to be the person who is really good at this Christianity stuff—the person others can look to as an example of righteousness. But as much as being the person who is the best Christian, who "follows Jesus" the most closely can feel a little seductive, it's simply never been who I am or who my parishioners need me to be. I'm not running after Jesus. Jesus is running *my* ass down. Yeah, I am a leader, but I'm leading them onto the street to get hit by the speeding bus of confession and absolution, sin and sainthood, death and resurrection—that is, the gospel of Jesus Christ. I'm a leader, but only by saying, "Oh, screw it. I'll go first."

I stood the next day in the copper light of sundown in the parish hall where House for All Sinners and Saints meets and confessed all of this to my congregation. I told them there had been a million reasons for me to want to be the prophetic voice for change, but every time I tried, I was confronted by my own bullshit. I told them I was unqualified to be an example of anything but needing Jesus.

That evening I admitted to my congregation that I had to look at how my outrage feels good for a while, but only like eating candy corn feels good for a while—I know it's nothing more than empty calories. My outrage feels empty because what I am desperate for is to speak the truth of my burden of sin and have Jesus take it from me, yet ranting about the system or about other people will always be my go-to instead. Because maybe if I show the right level of outrage, it'll make up for the fact that every single day of my life I have benefitted from the very same system that acquitted George Zimmerman. My opinions feel good until I crash from the self-righteous sugar high, then realize I'm still sick and hungry for a taste of mercy.

✢

The first time I was asked to give a lecture on preaching at the Festival of Homiletics, a national conference for preachers, they wanted me to give a talk on what preaching is like at House for All. I wasn't sure what to say, so I asked my congregation. There was passion in their replies, and none of it had to do with how much they appreciate their preacher being such an amazing role model for them. Not one of them said they love all the real-life applications they receive in the sermons for how to have a more victorious marriage. Almost all of them said they love that their preacher is so obviously preaching to herself and just allowing them to overhear it.

My friend Tullian put it this way: "Those most qualified to speak the gospel are those who truly know how unqualified they are to speak the gospel."

Never once did Jesus scan the room for the best example of holy living and send that person out to tell others about him. He always sent stumblers and sinners. I find that comforting.

4

✣

Whale Spit in the Superdome

Now the word of the LORD came to Jonah son of Amittai, saying, "Go at once to Nineveh, that great city, and cry out against
it; for their wickedness has come up before me." But Jonah set out
to flee to Tarshish from the presence of the LORD.

—JONAH 1:1–3

When the Lutheran denomination we are a part of invited me
to speak to thirty-five thousand teenagers and adults at their
2012 National Youth Gathering in New Orleans, I said no
thank you. I'd never seen teenagers as my audience, and I am
pretty sure that teenagers don't think I'm cool. Middle-aged people
think teenagers will think I'm cool, but that's different. Yes, I don't look
or behave like most respectable women in their midforties, but likely I
seem hip only to people older than me. I know this, and so I said no
thank you. Twice.

Besides, I don't have a "heart for the youth." Some people, like my
husband and my friend Kristen, love kids. But I'd simply rather not

spend time with teenagers (other than my own, who I adore and who make me laugh and who are amazing), and I'd rather not be in front of tens of thousands of them. Were I Jonah, youth events would be my Nineveh. I want to be a speaker only in Tarshish.

The Youth Gathering staff e-mailed back, "Oh no, Nadia, we never have youth ministry people as speakers on the main stage at these events. We've had sports celebrities, CNN heroes, Desmond Tutu. . . ."

To which I thought, *Desmond Tutu? Oh yeah, I'm always in line right behind that guy,* but instead I replied, "You're not exactly convincing me I'm the right person."

They came back with, "Well, we really want the first night of the gathering to start off with some good ole Lutheran theology. We seldom have actual Lutherans on the main stage, and we want the kids to begin this event by seeing a different image of what a Lutheran looks like, and with a strong message of grace."

Sucker punch. The Nineveh Tourism Council was winning. I said yes.

A few months after I accepted the invitation, I discovered that not everyone wanted me there. Nor did they want Pastor Andrena Ingram, an African American Lutheran pastor who is HIV-positive and a recovering addict, to have been invited to speak. Apparently, thousands of parents had been warned that their children would be exposed to dangerous ideas from scandalous women if we weren't uninvited. Of course if no one had ever been exposed to dangerous ideas from scandalous women, Christianity itself would not have had its unique beginning nor its glorious history, but whatever.

Although I felt that the youth of the Lutheran church were actually fairly safe in the care of Pastor Ingram and Pastor Bolz-Weber, this backlash didn't exactly eradicate my misgivings about speaking at a national youth event. At first it made me angry. So while trying to write my talk, I was distracted by how I might insert some kind of passive aggressive remark about how ridiculous some people are for thinking that my past and my personal style are somehow dangerous for today's youth. I had already been asked to not say any swear words in front of the kids—as though these teens had never heard the word *shit* before and would be irreparably scarred if they heard it from a pastor at a youth event. But, you know, fair enough.

The night before I left for New Orleans, I sat in my living room with my husband, Matthew, a pastor who has a lot of experience in youth work; my young son, Judah; and my daughter, Harper, a teenager herself. Needing a little extra confidence, I asked if they would give me some feedback on how I planned to open my talk.

I recited the opening lines: "Some people don't think I look very Lutheran because of the tattoos, but then I show them that I have the entire liturgical year inked on my left arm, Advent to Pentecost. I'm like, hey . . . you can't get more Lutheran than that!"

They all silently stared at me until I knew that only our family dog was on my side.

"Teenagers won't think that's funny," Matthew offered, "and they might not even know what you're talking about."

To which our daughter added, "Yeah, that's kinda dumb." (Okay, maybe I don't adore my own teens so much.)

I scowled, grabbed the dog's leash, and headed out the door for a walk, mainly so I could gather my wits and call friends who knew better than my husband and kids and could tell me my speech was awesome. Walking through my urban Denver neighborhood and nodding at the other passersby, I kept thinking, *I bet that woman over there walking out of her 1930s bungalow with her schnauzer isn't about to embarrass herself in front of tens of thousands of teenage Lutherans tomorrow.*

As soon as I was able to tame my self-pity, I called my friend Kristen and ran through my talk with her. She had been in youth ministry for over a decade and was kind enough to take my panicked call. Surely she could bolster my fading confidence.

"It sounds like you're talking to their parents. Here's what you might think about saying instead," and she outlined an entire message for me, all of which was solid and none of which was anything I would ever say. Freaking out, I just walked the dog faster and called my friend Shane, who had spoken at these large-scale youth gatherings before and, like myself, was not a "youth ministry person."

"Oh, honey, you *should* be scared. Teenagers are a rough audience."

Before going to bed that night, I remember thinking two things: (1) I'm going to eat it with a fork in front of thirty-five thousand people; (2) I need better friends. I lay awake, anticipating the deafening sound of the crowd not laughing at my opening. I spent most of that night fantasizing about ways to miss my plane, become ill, or have a nervous breakdown.

By the time I got on the plane early the next morning, I was sleep-deprived, filled with dread, and feeling as though I were about to give a talk in a foreign land without the aid of an interpreter. And then Chloe sat beside me. Like a foreign attaché from Nineveh.

I was too consumed by my own anxiety about the Youth Gathering and irritation at having to sit in the middle seat to notice the young teen coming down the aisle, dyed pink bangs hanging over her face like a protective visor, at once inviting and rejecting attention. She apologetically shuffled into the window seat next to me and pulled out a worn black backpack from which she grabbed an Anime comic and her sketch pad. Her shoulders turned in and down as though she were trying to hide what her pink bangs couldn't.

Shyly, and without making eye contact, she snuck a look at my bare arms and said, "Nice tattoos."

"Oh thanks. I like them. Which is good, since, you know, I'll have them for a while."

She smiled. I think. It was hard to tell.

We sat in silence again as the rest of the plane filled with travelers, many of whom were also on their way to our conference in New Orleans. (I knew this because they were wearing matching T-shirts from various Lutheran congregations, like Midwestern gang colors.)

"So, what are you drawing?" I asked her. She said it was Manga (Japanese-style animated figures) but that she also draws fantasy characters. I told her that my daughter, Harper, does the same thing. "You should tell her about this social media website where she can upload her art," Chloe offered. This all happened before takeoff, so I texted Harper the URL Chloe gave me and she texted back, "Yeah Mom, I know." (See? Not cool.)

Chloe kept drawing and hiding and peeking out to look at my tattoos again. "Did those hurt?" she asked, which was right around the time I noticed the shiny thin lines on her arms. *Not like those,* I thought to myself.

"Not so bad," I said instead, "but the one on the top of my foot . . . and a big one on my back, holy shit did those hurt!" She smiled.

"I want one, but I don't have the money," she said. She still wasn't looking at me.

"One day you will, and maybe then you'll be old enough not to get something stupid like I did when I was your age. What would you get if you *did* have the money?"

This started a long conversation, and by the time we were halfway to New Orleans, she was telling me about her life: not knowing who her dad was, the restraining order against her older sister who had hurt her badly last year. She talked about how stupid her school is and how they put her in special ed classes when in fact she's really good at math; she just thinks graphs are lame, so she refuses to fill them in. She was smart, I could tell. She just didn't fit in. I told her that my high school counselor was a complete bitch who thought I should go to trade school, and yet here I am with a graduate degree and a couple of published books to my name. So who's laughing now?

A smile forced itself onto her face like an uninvited guest and she immediately looked lighter and younger. For a second, she even looked me in the eye.

"So," I finally asked, "are you on your way to the Lutheran Youth Gathering?"

She looked at me, stunned. "Yeah . . . wait, are *you* going to the Lutheran Youth Gathering?"

I smiled and said, "Yeah . . . ends up, I'm a Lutheran pastor and I'm doing a thing there tomorrow night."

"Shut up!" she said, and I laughed. She told me that there are only a couple of girls in her youth group who even really talk to her and that she didn't want to come on this trip. She doesn't fit. I said I understood because I don't either.

We fell into silence, and I read my book and she worked on a drawing, which she gave to me when we landed. It was a Manga drawing of me.

She hugged me in the aisle of the 737 and thanked me for talking to her. And I thanked her for the drawing.

Sometimes I'm so thick that God has no choice but to be almost embarrassingly obtuse. Like sending me a hurting kid with glistening lines cut in her arm—a kid with protective pink bangs, a kid who doesn't fit, a kid who in her own way said to me, *Oh hey, God told me to tell you something: Get over yourself.*

✛

You can't really see the people you're talking to if the place from which you are talking happens to be a stage in the Superdome. The audience is so far away that there is really no way to see facial expressions or hear their laughter. It feels like doing radio. Well, like doing radio under lights so invasively bright that you start wondering if they are not stage lights at all but are, in fact, lights from an alien spacecraft about to beam you up. You just start talking like a blinded radio personality about to be abducted by aliens, all the while pretending to be speaking at a youth gathering, and you just hope for the best.

I had no idea if what I was saying from the faraway stage under what felt like alien tractor-beam lights was being received well, or if it was "working." But I did know to whom I was speaking, because right before walking out on stage, I looked at the piece of paper that was folded in my back pocket—the Manga drawing of myself. As I stood in front of tens of thousands of terrifying teenagers, I knew that I was just talking to Chloe, the girl who didn't fit.

So I told my story: a girl who didn't fit, raised fundamentalist Christian, left church, entered addiction, got clean, met nice Lutheran boy, became Lutheran, became Lutheran pastor, started church.

"Some of your parents and pastors were really upset that I was your speaker tonight," I said. "They thought someone with my past shouldn't be allowed to talk to thousands of teenagers. And you know what I have to say about that?" I paused. "They are absolutely right."

Silence. I took a deep breath and continued. "Somebody with my past of alcoholism and drug abuse and promiscuity and lying and stealing shouldn't be allowed to talk to you. But you know what? Somebody with my *present,* who I am *now,* shouldn't be allowed to either. I am a sarcastic, heavily tattooed, angry person who swears like a truck driver! I am a flawed person who really should not be allowed to talk to you. But you know what?" I asked. "That's the God we are dealing with, people!"

The kids went *nuts.* Clapping, screaming, on their feet, *nuts.*

Actually, I was floored. I had no idea they were even listening. It took a while for them to stop, and then I continued. "Let me tell you about this God." I told them that this is a God who has always used imperfect people, that this is a God who walked among us and who ate with all the wrong people and kissed lepers. I told them that this is a God who rose from the dead and grilled fish on the beach with his friends and then ascended to heaven and is especially present to us in the most offensively ordinary things: wheat, wine, water, words. I told them that this God has *never* made sense.

"And you don't need to either, because this God will use you, this God will use all of you, and not just your strengths, but your failures and your failings. Your weakness is fertile ground for a forgiving God to make something new and to make something beautiful, so don't ever think that all you have to offer are your gifts. *That's* what it looks like to be a Lutheran." *Chloe, you know what you are? You're a Lutheran. Like me.* Again, they went nuts.

Later, when I snuck back onto the floor of the Superdome to listen to the closing band, I was overtaken by kids. One girl in a pink hoodie two sizes too big was crying. "I'm fifteen years old, and you and I have kind of the same story, and I think you saved my life tonight." I hugged her and told her she was beautiful.

After hugging what felt like approximately all of the kids who were there that night, I found and hugged my husband, Matthew, who had flown in a couple of hours earlier to offer support for his crazy wife who was worried about talking to teenagers. We drove through a rainstorm back to our hotel and sat in the stillness of our room, quietly eating the steak I ordered to still my raging postadrenaline hunger.

"What just happened?" I asked Matthew.

Not even looking up from his dinner, he just said, "You can talk to teenagers."

Despite my desire to flee to the comforts of Tarshish, a land of grownups who get my jokes and (just maybe) think I'm cool, I had been spat up onto the shores of teenager Nineveh, and wiping the whale spit off of myself, I spoke God's assignment to me and survived. Sometimes the fact that there is nothing about you that makes you the right person to do something is exactly what God is looking for.

I *still* get e-mails and tweets and messages and handwritten letters from those kids on a regular basis. I can't make the math work. There is no way to take whatever skill I may have as a public speaker plus the work I put into that talk (very little, actually) and have it add up to what happened. Yet I'm slowly beginning to understand that when the math doesn't work, we are walking in a place outside of logic and cause and effect. Some people call that Holy Ground.

We come dangerously close to spiritual self-flattery when we say,

"God used me to do something." But perhaps the opposite is true too. We flatter ourselves just as much when we claim that we can't do the hard things God sets before us.

Without higher-quality material to work with, God resorts to working through us for others and upon us through others. Those are some weirdly restorative, disconcerting shenanigans to be caught up in: God forcing God's people to see themselves as God sees them, to do stuff they know they are incapable of doing, so that God might make use of them, and make them to be both humble recipients and generous givers of grace, so that they may be part of God's big project on earth, so that they themselves might find unexpected joy through surprising situations.

So that pastors on planes might be reminded by girls with pink bangs and glistening scars to get over themselves.

5

You Are Not "The Blessing"

"I was hungry and you gave me food, I was thirsty and you gave me something to drink, I was a stranger and you welcomed me, I was naked and you gave me clothing, I was sick and you took care of me, I was in prison and you visited me." Then the righteous will answer him, "Lord, when was it that we saw you hungry and gave you food, or thirsty and gave you something to drink? And when was it that we saw you a stranger and welcomed you, or naked and gave you clothing? And when was it that we saw you sick or in prison and visited you?" And the king will answer them, "Truly I tell you, just as you did it to one of the least of these who are members of my family, you did it to me."

— MATTHEW 25:35–40

The air conditioning in the Orlando Marriott ballroom where we were meeting had been taking itself way too seriously all week long. We were there as a denomination (the Evangelical Lutheran Church in America) to try again to take Jesus at his word when, in Matthew 25, he says that when we clothe the naked and feed the hungry we do so to Christ's own self.

The ELCA gets together every couple of years to figure stuff like this out.

This year—2011—we had been debating whether or not to pass the denomination's proposed statement on human genetics and genetic research. I knew we were there to undertake serious work, but I was feeling cranky, mostly on account of that air conditioner. I was so cold and tired that I began to fantasize the National Guard would show up with blankets and bottled water since I basically experience any kind of physical discomfort as a crisis.

But then—right before we moved to the adjoining ballroom for worship, and right after I had finished eating all the peanut M&M's that sat in a Styrofoam paper cup in front of me at my synod's table, and right before I was just about to start in on my neighbor's candy, and right after I felt annoyed about the session going overtime—my reality check began.

At that moment, a forty-something, disturbingly thin, very gray-skinned woman in a head scarf stepped up to the microphone to speak in support of the social statement that provided an ethical framework for genetics testing and stem-cell research. The whole room shifted into focus. She told us that she had stage 4 cancer—a cancer related to a genetic disease—and she begged us to adopt the social statement on genetics that we were about to vote on.

"While it is too late for me," she said, as a quiet room of over a thousand people seemed to stop breathing for a minute, "I am so grateful for a church that is willing to ask difficult questions and make bold statements in support of continuing genetic research and that our God can indeed work in, with, and under medical science."

Because, she continued, while she was not long for this world, she hoped the work of geneticists would produce a miracle someday so that others like her might not die at such a young age.

The silence that followed her two short minutes at the microphone felt holy and grave and gave us all a moment to grab tissues. Mercifully it also happened to be the exact time we were scheduled to break for our daily Eucharist (an even better rescue in my book than the National Guard with blankets and water).

Fifteen minutes later, I sat on one of the twelve hundred cushioned chairs that were awkwardly arranged for a liturgy below sparkly chandeliers in the fluorescent wash of the hotel conference space.

My row was still empty when Bruce, a handsome bishop in his late fifties, walked by. Grateful for a familiar face, I caught his eye, patted the chair next to me, and gave him a churchy "come hither" look. We'd met the night before at a reception, at which he had approached me about speaking at an event the following fall. I wanted to say no, because, well, I almost always want to say no to everything, but since he was snarky funny, I said yes. I am defenseless against snarky funny bishops.

I dug out a scarf from my bag and made a remark about the fucking air conditioning as we listened to the prelude for the service to follow, and by "listened to," I mean made fun of. "Bruce, is this prelude helping us or hurting us, you think?"

There is something about dropping F-bombs and making fun of worship music with a bishop that makes me feel warm and fuzzy.

But the feeling wasn't to last very long.

Before he could answer my dumb question, a woman in her sixties walked up and placed an envelope in his hand. She looked serious, making me feel even worse for jumping to shit-talking so soon after everyone had been deeply moved by the testimony of a woman with cancer.

"This is from all the other bishops' spouses," she said to him with tears in her eyes. "Tell her we love her and are praying for her. Honestly, after that last speaker, we all wanted to vote right then to approve the genetics statement."

I looked away and felt that particular discomfort you feel when you're present at something far too personal for a new acquaintance. What do I do? Ignore it? If he were hungry and I were trying to be a Matthew 25 kind of Christian, I'd know to give him something to eat, and if he were naked, well, the hotel security would have already escorted him out. But he was grieving. How might I be Christ to him?

"Bruce," I finally said after the woman left, "is your wife sick?" It's the kind of question that has to be asked while maintaining eye contact even if you feel like you'd rather just disappear.

It took him a few minutes of looking at his knees before he looked in my eyes. And when he did, he said, "Yes. Just three weeks ago she was diagnosed with stage 4 lung cancer, which has spread to her liver."

So there I was. What was I gonna do? There was no way I was going to presume to start pastoring a bishop I had just barely met. I was relieved that the organ music started, saving me from having to figure out what to say.

As the liturgy went on, I sat there selfishly distracted by what felt like the complete unsingability of the opening hymn when I realized that this bishop sitting next to me was also not singing. He was weeping. And in that moment it didn't matter that he was a bishop and I a pastor with a bad attitude. I put my arm around him and just kept singing—and I tried to sing that hymn I never would have chosen even

louder. I sang louder because my brother in Christ couldn't sing himself. I had to sing for us both. And then I took his hand.

After the liturgy, I asked Bruce if he would like me to pray for
him and anoint him with oil.[5] His eyes teared up and he said, "Thank
you, yes."

I committed to pray for him every day after that and did so over the
course of the next nine weeks, until the untimely death of his wife. During those nine weeks, I prayed and checked in regularly via phone, text
message, and e-mail. In some way, Bruce leaned on me, sending really
honest text messages about how much pain he was in or how hard it was.

Years ago, after pagers were popular but before cell phones came
around, my parents' church had prayer pagers that were carried by people going through crisis. Folks at church would have the pager number,
and every time they prayed for the person who had just lost a loved one
or who was going through a difficult course of chemo, that person
would feel the pager buzz with each prayer offered. This always stayed
with me as a powerful idea, so I tried to let Bruce know, with some
regularity, that I was praying for him.

As the days passed and his wife grew increasingly ill, the messages
continued. "Just prayed for you," I'd text or e-mail, and he'd inevitably
answer with "Thanks. This is so hard. I'm not sure how to do this."

"You'll do it," I'd reply, "but it will feel like shit and it won't be
easy."

What else could I say that wouldn't be complete nonsense? If nothing else, I admired his honesty and his ability to reach out for support.

---

5. "Are any among you suffering? They should pray. Are any cheerful? They should sing songs
of praise. Are any among you sick? They should call for the elders of the church and have
them pray over them, anointing them with oil in the name of the Lord. The prayer of faith
will save the sick, and the Lord will raise them up; and anyone who has committed sins will
be forgiven. Therefore confess your sins to one another, and pray for one another, so that you
may be healed. The prayer of the righteous is powerful and effective" (James 5:13–16).

The morning after Cynthia died, I received a call from someone in Bruce's office letting me know the funeral would be held near where they live in Madison, Wisconsin. Getting on the plane a few days later, I wondered what I was doing attending a funeral for a woman I'd never met. Yet I had made a promise to care about her husband, and so that night when Bruce approached me at the funeral reception and asked if I would stay until everyone had left, I said yes. As we stood in an empty church fellowship hall next to the drained coffee pots and empty cheese trays, I asked, "So, Bruce, who pastors bishops?"

"No one," he said in almost a whisper, not out of secrecy or shame but out of the weighty truth of it.

On the drive back to the house of my friends Jay and Annie, where I was staying the night in Milwaukee, I thought about what Bruce had said, and it made me think that maybe we simply don't want our leaders to have needs. Maybe it's not only the leaders who think they should be perfect; maybe it's also their followers who expect them to have it all together. Maybe we want the people who care for us and lead us to not be like us, to not struggle like us, because if we realize they, too, are hurting and needy, then maybe the spell—the illusion that we're okay, that we're in good hands—breaks. Like how distressed I was when I saw Miss Kramer, my third grade teacher, walking out of the teachers' bathroom. *Wait. You mean teachers also go to the bathroom? You mean, like me?* I never saw her the same again.

I drove in the dark through small town Wisconsin thinking about how I had inadvertently become one of Bishop Bruce's pastors during the time of his wife's death, and how it was an honor, but that if I was totally honest, I also felt some kind of weird pride about it. He is easy to love and I was happy to get to be one of the people who, in a small way, was able to help carry him through. We call this kind of thing "serving others" as though it's an entirely selfless thing, but to tell the truth, I've never known how to keep from feeling self-important when I help people. Being the one who gets to serve is a position of power. No matter how selfless I'd like to think I am, there's always something in it for me—even if it's the satisfaction of knowing I am a good Matthew 25 Christian, that I am "being Christ" to someone else.

While we as people of God are certainly called to feed the hungry and clothe the naked, that whole "we're blessed to be a blessing" thing can still be kind of dangerous. It can be dangerous when we self-importantly place ourselves above the world, waiting to descend on those below so we can be the "blessing" they've been waiting for, like it or not. Plus, seeing myself as the blessing can pretty easily obscure the way in which I am actually part of the problem and can hide the ways in which I, too, am poor and needing care. Seeing myself or my church or my denomination as "the blessing"—like so many mission trips to help "those less fortunate than ourselves"—can easily descend into a blend of benevolence and paternalism. We can start to see the "poor" as supporting characters in a big story about how noble, selfless, and helpful we are.

After meeting Bruce and struggling with what it means to be the hands and feet of Christ in the world when I am so prone to pride, I looked harder at Matthew 25 and realized that if Jesus said "I was hungry and you fed me," then Christ's presence is not embodied in those who feed the hungry (as important as that work is), but Christ's presence is in the hungry being fed. Christ comes not in the form of those who visit the imprisoned but in the imprisoned being cared for. And to be clear, Christ does not come to us *as* the poor and hungry. Because, as anyone for whom the poor are not an abstraction but actual flesh-and-blood people knows, the poor and hungry and imprisoned are not a romantic special class of Christlike people. And those who meet their needs are not a romantic special class of Christlike people. We all are equally as sinful and saintly as the other. No, Christ comes to us in the *needs* of the poor and hungry, needs that are met by another so that the gleaming redemption of God might be known.

No one gets to play Jesus. But we do get to experience Jesus in that holy place where we meet others' needs and have our own needs met. We are all the needy and the ones who meet needs. To place ourselves or anyone else in only one category is to lie to ourselves.

Of this much I am sure: I wasn't the one who allowed Christ to be revealed in the encounter of the sarcastic pastor and the weeping bishop. It was Bruce's need that revealed Christ. Bruce didn't get to play Jesus and neither did I, but Bruce did allow himself to bear a need that someone else could, however imperfectly, meet. And when the grief of our brother was cared about, Jesus was cared about.

The fact is, we are all, at once, bearers of the gospel and receivers of it. We meet the needs of others and have our needs met. And the strangeness of the good news is that, like those in Matthew 25 who sat before the throne and said *Huh? When did we ever feed you, Lord?*, we never know when we experience Jesus in all of this. All that we have is a promise, a promise that our needs are holy to God. A promise that Jesus is present in the meeting of needs and that his kingdom is here. But he's a different kind of king who rules over a different kind of kingdom. Being part of Christ's bizarro kingdom looks more like being thirsty and having someone you don't even like give you water than it looks like polishing your crown. It looks more like giving my three extra coats to the trinity of junkies on the corner than it looks like ermine-trimmed robes.

That is the surprising scandal of the gospel, the surprising scandal of the kingdom: it looks like the same crappy mess that bumps us out of our unconscious addiction to being good, so that we can look at Jesus as he approaches us on the street and says, *Man, you look like you could use a good meal.*

The Lord be with you.
And also with you.
Let us give thanks to the Lord our God.
It is right to give our thanks and praise.

6

A Thief in the Night

When Jim and his boyfriend, Stuart, showed up to church the first Sunday of Advent 2008, there were only about thirty of us in our small band of Jesus-y misfits. Just that Sunday, we had started to gather weekly, rather than monthly, for Eucharist. Jim and Stuart have been part of House for All Sinners and Saints ever since, even though the last thing Jim wanted in his life at the time was church. A sentiment to which I can completely relate.

Both in their early forties, Jim is fashionably bald, ginger-bearded, and pretty understated, while Stuart is a tall, funny, and larger than life occasional drag queen. I loved them immediately because even on their very first Sunday they helped carry the seemingly countless Rubbermaid containers of our church junk upstairs to the little closet where all our church's belongings were stored, and I'm a sucker for anyone who is helpful at putting stuff away.

The next Sunday Jim and Stuart came back. After church Jim slid into the vinyl booth next to me at Sputnik, which at the time was the postliturgy bar of choice for House for All.

"I'm so glad you guys came again this week," I said, trying to sound welcoming but not creepy. "Yeah," Jim replied. "This afternoon Stuart said, 'Let's go back to that House for All Sinners and Saints,' and I was like, 'Ugh. Seriously?'"

I laughed out loud because he told me the truth. I thought it was hysterical that someone would sit across from the pastor, order a beer, and say how he hadn't wanted to come back to that pastor's church. The best part was that after I laughed, he didn't try to back-pedal. He just laughed with me and added, "I'm not so into church right now."

"I get it," I said. And then we moved on to other conversations, mostly involving recent movies and then about fifteen minutes of Jim explaining to me how to get my mail accounts to sync on my iPhone.

Later I would learn that Jim had very good reason to "not be into" church. During a nine-year period when he was struggling with his identity, Jim had worked on the staff at a premier Evangelical megachurch outside of Chicago, which had actually been a refreshing change from what Jim had been immersed in as a child. He was raised a conservative Baptist. And after I learned about his upbringing, I knew why, on that first week that he and Stuart had come to worship, he squirmed through the reading of the gospel, a reading that included lines like, "some will be taken." I could see him shifting his feet, crossing his arms, and I think I even heard him sigh. Of course, Jim was raised in a church that believed in "the rapture."

I myself had never heard of the rapture until I was well into my thirties. My fundamentalist upbringing was simply too "Bible-believing" to go in for that particular brand of crazy, since the rapture was an idea that some preacher in the UK came up with in the late nineteenth century. When it comes down to it, folks can take a couple of verses in the Bible and run any direction they want with them, including the direction of a multimillion dollar publishing deal, if you're Tim LaHaye (author of the *Left Behind* book series with Jerry

B. Jenkins). Sure, there are a couple of references to *some being taken and some not,* but in my reading of it, the rapture itself is not really in the Bible.

I am certain there are more gracious ways of explaining the rapture, and not everyone who believes in it fits this description, but to believe in the rapture feels to me like it's the same as believing that when Jesus comes back, he will do so as a judgmental, angry bastard who apparently underwent a total personality transplant since his resurrection. Or as a selective magician who will make all the good people float up to the sky like a million Evangelical Mary Poppinses and force the bad people to be "left behind" on earth to suffer terribly.

There are some Christians who talk about the rapture as if the good people in heaven will be given these awesome box seats from which to watch the bad people suffer on earth. This is the good people's reward for never having any fun while in this earthly existence. This sort of fear-mongering bullshit sells like hot cakes. People eat it up. And why wouldn't we? It panders to the selfish, hateful, vengeance-seeking parts of ourselves, like God himself is cosigning on it all. Which, come to think of it, is what so much bad religion does for us.

So needless to say, rapture theories are nothing I've ever taken very seriously. But Jim was raised with them, and in his first week at House for All, he shifted his feet through the gospel reading about people being snatched out of fields and God coming like a "thief in the night." *A Thief in the Night,* I discovered, also happens to be the title of a 1970s low-budget made-for-Christians movie that scared the bejesezus out of an entire generation of children who, like Jim, believed what the adults in their life told them: that, at any minute, everyone they loved could be taken to heaven by Jesus, and if they were bad (like if maybe they were gay, or had felt up their girlfriend, or drunk a beer, or stolen a candy bar, or said "Goddamnit" when they got a D on their geography quiz) they would be "left behind" with the other bad people to be tormented for eternity.

"I would come home from school and my mom would still be at the store and if I couldn't see anyone else on my block I'd get panicky, thinking they were gone and that I was left behind," Jim later explained to me. "And I'd basically have an anxiety attack until my mom came home. When she got there, I couldn't even tell her why I was so upset because then she'd start to ask what I had done to deserve to be left behind." Many of my other parishioners confessed to me this kind of fear the religion of their childhood had instilled in them.

I had little idea how many of the thirty people present on that first Sunday of Advent were carrying around this kind of rapture PTSD when they walked into church and stomped the snow off their boots. And as a new preacher (I had been ordained for just over a week), I was unaware of the fact that in the first couple of weeks of Advent, the lectionary[6] doesn't actually address the story of Jesus's birth. There are no angels or mangers the first couple of weeks of Advent. Instead, we get apocalyptic texts. Weird, embarrassing, end-of-time stuff I'd quickly toss under sofa cushions if non-Christians stopped by for a visit and judged me as batshit crazy before I could tell them that apocalyptic texts were really common at the time the Bible was written. They were, like, available at the supermarket checkout line next to the celebrity magazines.

Apocalyptic texts were often code for speaking about the world the people at that time lived in; they were a way for people in politically

---

6. The lectionary is a set of assigned readings for each Sunday, which includes a psalm, a Hebrew Bible text (or one from Acts during Easter), and a reading each from the epistles and the Gospels.

dangerous situations to speak the truth about power—they were more commentary than prediction. And, yes, they are disturbing texts, but partly because they represent a genre we just aren't familiar with. Sort of like if sci-fi ceased being a genre two thousand years from now but *Battlestar Galactica* was still able to be seen, and the people in the year 4000, rather than understanding it to be a commentary about hubris and what it means to be human, saw it as a prediction of the future and waited around staring at the sky anticipating Cylon attacks. That doesn't mean all apocalyptic texts are invalidated because of genre, but it does mean that they're not meant to be crystal balls.

Here's the apocalyptic doozy I ended up reading on that first Sunday Jim visited:

> But about that day and hour no one knows, neither the angels of
> heaven, nor the Son, but only the Father. . . . Then two will be
> in the field; one will be taken and one will be left. . . . Keep
> awake therefore, for you do not know on what day your Lord is
> coming. But understand this: if the owner of the house had
> known in what part of the night the thief was coming, he would
> have stayed awake and would not have let his house be broken
> into. Therefore you also must be ready, for the Son of Man is
> coming at an unexpected hour. (Matthew 24:36, 40, 42–44)

In other words, I had to preach on a text that my friend Russell describes as "the anticipated threat of Jesus kidnapping someone at work and then breaking into my house and robbing me."

The weird thing about that little passage from Matthew is that it has been used by so many as a prediction of the end times or as an all-encompassing field guide for how to be ready for Jesus's return—how to know for sure that you will be raptured and not left behind. But given the number of incorrect end-times predictions there have been over the centuries—hell, even in my lifetime—there may be more to be learned by reading texts like this as descriptive and not predictive. If we are looking for certainty about the future from the Bible, this might be just about the worst place in the world to look for it.

No one knows, the text indicates. The angels don't know, Jesus doesn't know, you don't know. If the guy knew when the thief was coming he wouldn't have gotten his stuff stolen. So be ready because it's unexpected.

But how the heck can you be ready for something you don't know is coming? How can we be ready for the unexpected? Well, we can't.

So maybe being awake and alert and expectant—all themes of Advent—has nothing to do with knowing or certainty or prediction, but has a lot to do with being in a state of *un*knowing. My instinct is always to use my knowingness—my certainty I'm right, like how I am so clearly 100 percent right about the rapture being a made-up thing—as a sort of loss-prevention program, a system by which I protect myself from the unknown and the unexpected. Which works approximately none of the time. Perhaps like how Jim was certain he never wanted anything to do with church ever again.

Here's the thing: like the house owner, knowing what to look for as a way of avoiding being robbed is only advantageous if we assume being robbed is a bad thing. But perhaps having an unknowing brain allows us to be taken unaware by the grace of God, which is like a thief in the night. Maybe it's good news that Jesus has been staking the joint and there will be a break-in. The promise of Advent is that in the absence of knowing everything, we get robbed. There was and is and will be a break-in because God is not interested in our loss-prevention programs but in saving us from ourselves and saving us from our culture and saving us even from our certainties about God's story itself.

This holy thief *wants* to steal from us, and maybe that is literal and metaphoric at the same time. Perhaps, during Advent, a season with pornographic levels of consumption in which our credit card debts rise and our waistbands expand, the idea that Jesus wants to break in and jack some of our stuff is really good news. There's just a whole lot of crap in my house—again, both literally and metaphorically—that I could well do without.

So on that Sunday in 2008 when, despite his shifting feet and desire to not be in church, Jim came to House for All to listen to me preach, I suggested that maybe we should start making Advent lists—they'd be like Christmas lists, but instead of listing things we want Santa to bring us, we could write down things we want Christ to break in and take from us. In the hopes he could pickpocket the stupid junk in our houses, or abscond with our self-loathing or resentment . . . maybe break in in the middle of the night and take off with our compulsive eating or our love of money. That's how God works sometimes. Not through the things we are prepared for but through the things we don't expect.

I've mentioned before that it's tricky to try to speak of the way in which God moves in the world. It's been done so poorly and for such self-aggrandizing reasons by so many, myself included. I'm not sure I trust myself enough to feel confident in declaring that God is involved in something, especially if it's my own project. But I can pretty consistently see God in retrospect. I mean, in any given moment I am so filled with doubt and self-interest and ambition and neurosis that it's hard to be tuned in to God. But *after* something surprising or intensely beautiful happens, usually in spite of me and my machinations, *then* I begin to suspect God. God is the suspect, the thief.

Apocalyptic texts try to explain the present by injecting the present into the future. Like if, in order to talk in code about the Tea Party, I wrote a *Battlestar Gallactica* episode where the crew of the ship were slowly taken over by Cylons who wanted to privatize the fuel production onboard.

But I'm not going to do that. I can't actually project what is happening now into the future. I am terrible at predictions. But I *can* stand in the present and puzzle at what happened in the past. I can take depositions, give my own testimony. I can ask other people about their lives, try to make sense of what has happened. And whenever the evidence doesn't make any sense, I know exactly who to suspect. It's Jesus. Again.

Like when Diane, a young mom in my congregation who has a mentally unstable and emotionally abusive mother, e-mailed me and said, "The weirdest thing just happened. My mom posted on Facebook about what a hard time she is having and, well, you know . . . the stuff she usually posts, and she ended it by saying that she still feels God's love and presence. Normally this would have sent me into a mini-rage about how delusional and self-obsessed she is, but that didn't happen, Nadia. Strangely my first response to reading her post was *Of course she feels God's love and presence. That's just God's nature.* It's disorienting to not have the same resentment toward her that I've held on to for so long. But I think, having heard that message of God's love so much at church, that I believed it for myself and maybe I believe it so much for myself that I even believe it for my *mother*."

Maybe the blessed exchange I talked about earlier means that Jesus is skulking around like the Grinch after having stolen other people's

stuff, heavy laden with a huge red sack of our resentments and resistances and a bunch of other junk we never manage to get rid of ourselves no matter how much we know we should. Maybe he's just going
from one person to the next taking off with our useless trash.

✦

"So why do you wear that priest's shirt?" Jim asked me. We were in
Amy Clifford's living room at a Christmas party, and it had been three
weeks since Jim and Stuart had shown up at House for All. His expression said, "I'm on to you, so don't try to pull anything."

The food laid out next to us was charmingly southern, just like our
host. I grabbed a "forever amber"—a coconut/orange slice concoction
that is rolled into little balls—and popped it into my mouth before
realizing it was a very chewing-intensive food, thus making the time
between Jim's question and my answer awkwardly long.

As soon as my jaws were free, I explained to Jim that my shirt represents an office I hold when I preach and preside at communion and
that a clergy collar also represents the church's catholicity and the Lutheran tradition of which I am a part, that I'm not playing dress-up or
pretend.

Only after shutting up did I realize that using the word *catholic*
was perhaps a misstep. His skeptical look faded slightly only after a
good twenty minutes of safe conversation about TV binge watching,
and then perhaps only because the ham and biscuits arrived like the last
act in a Tennessee culinary drama.

For months after that first Sunday, Jim had insisted that, despite his
weekly attendance at liturgy and his technical and design work on behalf of the community (like designing an amazing poster for our Blessing of the Bicycles that included a bicycle chain around the sacred heart

of Jesus) he would not claim to be doing anything other than "hanging out" at House for All. He was not a member.

Of course we technically didn't have any members, but that's okay. Jim was there. And he kept coming back because the unexpected had happened: Jim had been certain that church was no longer for him, and this certainty worked for him for a while. But eventually, it was as though God broke in like a thief in an Advent night and stole it. Jim knew what to expect in a church that rejects him. He walked into our church with that expectation, and then he was robbed.

Welcome to Advent, Jim. But check your pockets before you leave.

7

Mary, Mother of Our Lord

The angel said to her, "Do not be afraid, Mary, for you have found favor with God. And now, you will conceive in your womb and bear a son, and you will name him Jesus. He will be great, and will be called the Son of the Most High, and the Lord God will give to him the throne of his ancestor David. He will reign over the house of Jacob forever, and of his kingdom there will be no end." Mary said to the angel, "How can this be, since I am a virgin?" The angel said to her, "The Holy Spirit will come upon you, and the power of the Most High will overshadow you; therefore the child to be born will be holy; he will be called Son of God. And now, your relative Elizabeth in her old age has also conceived a son; and this is the sixth month for her who was said to be barren. For nothing will be impossible with God." Then Mary said, "Here am I, the servant of the Lord; let it be with me according to your word." Then the angel departed from her.

— LUKE 1:30–38

W hen I was twelve-years-old, before the Great Cynicism of early adulthood took hold, I went to a school friend's house for a sleepover. It was winter, and when I entered into the lived-in kitchen of their seventies split-level home with my tote bag of fleece jammies and a spare toothbrush, I walked into what felt like a theological crime scene.

"Cassie, have you opened the Advent calendar today?" my friend's mom asked. Her mom had cancer and wore a thin brown scarf over her head. Hanging on the wall next to the avocado-colored refrigerator was something I was unprepared for and quietly scandalized by. The object in question revealed something shocking about Cassie and her family. No, they weren't heroin addicts or part of an armed militia. They. Were. Catholic.

And they weren't even trying to hide it. A cardboard calendar covered with images of Mary hung from the wall. Cassie walked toward it, opened up a little hinged square numbered 18 and handed me the single glossy piece of chocolate from inside in the shape of a bell. The pleasure of the waxy chocolate melting in my mouth was tempered by the feeling of pity for her mom, combined with scandal that couldn't have been stronger if the pictures on that Advent calendar had been of *Playboy* pinups. But don't get me wrong; I totally still ate the chocolate.

I knew Catholics existed, with their saints and candles and rosaries, and all their other exotic ways of being wrong. But now I had Catholic *friends*. And I couldn't stop staring at their Mary. She seemed luminescent and good and trustworthy and beautiful. And I was secretly jealous they got to have her.

I had no clue, of course, that Advent was a season and not just the name of scandalous chocolate-bearing pagan calendars that count down to Christmas. In fact, since at least the fifth century the four-week period before Christmas has been set aside in the church as a time of anticipation, waiting, and hope. But I would not know this, much less experience it, until decades after eating shiny Catholic chocolate.

Church of Christ kids like me, in Colorado Springs in 1982, did not have Advent calendars. No Sunday at our church was different from any other Sunday during the year, and that included Christmas, since Christmas was a cultural and not a religious holiday—because, for us, there were no religious holidays. Religious holidays were celebrated by people who didn't really believe in the Bible, because the Bible never said we should celebrate things like Advent and Christmas. (The Bible also never said we should brush our teeth or watch fireworks on the Fourth of July or breathe oxygen, yet that never seemed to bother the grownups at church.) So we kept Christ out of Christmas. Rudolph and Santa were fair game—but a nativity in the house? No way.

Actually, growing up, I don't remember hearing a lot about Jesus in general, apart from how horrible we should feel about being responsible for the fact that God had to kill him. But in all fairness, Jesus very well could have been mentioned more than that; I wasn't very good at paying attention during church.

Or at church retreats, like the one I attended just weeks after discovering Cassie's Catholic-ness. It was snowing outside the mountain lodge where we kids were all sitting on the cold floor listening to the speaker. I remember staring out at the beautiful snowfall, the right side of my face warmed by the fire next to me. The speaker paced back and forth holding an open Bible in one hand, its soft leather cover draping over each side of his hand like a rag. His wet boots left dark prints on the wood floor; the closer his footprints were to the fire, the faster they disappeared.

His main point was that God was waiting to see if we were grateful enough about Jesus's crucifixion that we would start living in a very particular way. The implication was that God was waiting to see if we did not use swear words, or lie about anything, or listen to rock music, or have any kind of sexual inclination toward someone of the opposite sex before we were married. God was waiting to see if we were always cheerful and never drank alcohol or were snarky. Then we would become worthy of God's favor.

"How would you be living," the man with the floppy Bible and wet boots asked us, "if you really believed?"

This type of teaching was standard fare at Christian youth retreats across the country. "Good" behavior equals godliness. But as I sat there, distracted by the evaporating footprints on the wooden floor, I kept thinking about Cassie's Mary calendar and wondered if the mother of Jesus was considered "good." After all, she got knocked up before she got married.

Mary got precious little mention in my religious upbringing apart from our sneering at people (like Roman Catholics) who "worshiped" her. To us, Mary was little more than a minor character in the Christmas story and to pay any more attention to her than that was to inch dangerously toward Catholic idolatry. Sure, Mary could be admired for her obedience, but we knew better than to turn Mary into some kind of golden calf—that which the mistaken, the lost, and the ignorant worship instead of God.

I now realize that one fabulous advantage to observing the church year is that it throws Mary in our face every single December and January. She won't be ignored. Which I think is awesome. I knew when I saw her in Cassie's home, on the Advent calendar and on paintings and little statues, that I loved her, that I wanted her strength and beauty. And perhaps like a sheltered adolescent's same-sex attraction, I bottled it up and forgot it as best I could. After that night of being transfixed by Cassie's Mary, I didn't pick up my love of Our Lady again until my twenties, when I had left the Church of Christ and had sought meaning and community elsewhere. So when I eventually returned to the Christian faith, I did so with a passion for and devotion to Mary in tow—which eventually demonstrated itself in Virgin Mary belt buckles, tattoos, and medallions hanging from the rearview mirror of my car.

I may have found inspiration in the form of the Blessed Virgin Mary, but looking around my new Lutheran home, I realized that many mainline Protestants don't really know what to do with Mary. It's like Roman Catholics have dibs on her and we just kind of stand by, only dusting her off once a year to be the pretty young girl in the nativity set and then putting her quickly away before she embarrasses anyone. Which is sad because there are so many reasons to love Mary.

She has been loved for centuries for being "good," the docile picture of purity and virginity. As a matter of fact, some church doctrines have been written to say that unlike other women, Mary was born without sin. Which, of course, implies that God could never choose to make God's home in the womb of an *actual* woman, since we know that actual women are sinful, fleshy temptresses. So Mary had to have been a special one-off who was really, really different from all the other tramps out there. And so it was her really, really differentness from actual women that earned her God's favor.

In contrast, Mary has also been loved by leftists in the church as a sort of first-century teenage female Che Guevara, since in Luke 1 she sings the Magnificat, a song that includes images of God overthrowing the social order, feeding the hungry, and sending the rich away empty-handed. I like this image of Mary as a political revolutionary, even while I am sure it's slightly misguided since the Prince of Peace's mom wouldn't be a guerilla with a side arm strapped to her leg and a Kalashnikov in her blessed arms.

Others, folks not drawn to religion, or those who, like atheists, are largely repelled by it, seem disturbed by the irrationality of the whole thing. For them, Mary, and especially the Virgin Birth, is a fairy tale for the gullible, something ignorant people believe in because they haven't learned to use human reason or listen to NPR as much as they should.

I just don't feel satisfied with any of the above. But I want a way to view Mary and even the Christmas story itself without sentimentality *or* cynicism.

So . . . here we have a girl, likely between thirteen and fifteen years of age. She's a peasant and she's engaged to a pretty religious guy. An angelic figure visits her saying that she's found favor with God and is going to conceive a son by the Holy Spirit and that this child will be holy and will sit on David's throne—none of which seems terribly likely to be true, given her socioeconomic status.

When we think about the Annunciation, the scene between the angel Gabriel and Mary and how he told her these outrageous things, we think of the faith it took for her to believe that the Holy Spirit really would knock her up and that her son, the illegitimate child of an insignificant girl, really would have a throne and a kingdom. But I wonder: If I had been in her place, which would be harder for me to believe? The part about being knocked up by God and giving birth to a king? Or the part where the angel said I was favored? I mean, if an angel came to me and said, "Greetings, favored one," I'd be like, "You've got the wrong girl." There's no way I would trust that the angel meant me. You know, since I've never managed to have my life *look* the way the youth minister implied it should in order to earn God's favor.

"What would your lives look like if you really believed?" said the man with the floppy Bible. As a twelve-year-old, I believed. At least I *thought* I believed, but no matter how hard I tried, I just never seemed to be able to make myself into something worthy of God's favor. Perhaps if I had a personality more naturally predisposed toward clean living and clean speaking and clean thinking I could have pulled it off, but as it was I was just me and all the guilt-tripping in the world never seemed to change that. So instead I paid attention to the snow and the warmth of my cheek. I tuned out the youth minister in wet boots preaching to me about how my life should look. Because I just couldn't muster up a *yes* to what seemed like God's conditional *maybe* toward me.

But here's where Mary had some real chops. She heard outrageous things from an angel and said, "Let it be with me according to your word" (Luke 1:38). Mary trusted the word from the angel, telling her that she was favored. And maybe that trust is what *made* her favored. We don't know the details of her life, but I like to think that she was a normal girl with all the struggles and inconsistencies that come with being a normal girl. Maybe the really outrageous act of faith on Mary's part was trusting that she had found favor with God. I may feel used to the idea that if I live a certain kind of life, I can make myself worthy of God. But what if God's Word is so much more powerful than our ability to become worthy of God? I mean, not for nothing, but if God can create the universe by speaking it into existence, then I think God can make us into God's beloved by simply saying it is so. This, it seems to me, is a vital and overlooked miracle of the Annunciation story.

We have no idea what Mary was like before the angel visited her, but here's what I'm thinking: I seriously doubt that she made herself into a girl whom God could favor because she took the advice of her youth rabbi and lived the way she should. If the way God seems to favor prostitutes and tax collectors and adulterous kings over the smug, righteous, and powerful is any indication, then I think it's safe to assume that it is God's nature to look upon young peasant girls with favor. Because God's just like that. At least that's how we see God consistently acting in the Bible.

What that youth minister at the retreat essentially was asking was how "good" we would be if we felt awful enough about how God had to kill Jesus because we were bad. But I didn't realize that until my parishioner Stephen said something years later.

Stephen looks like an aging movie star, is the VP at a Fortune 500 company, is a statewide elected official, lives in a loft downtown, and is still a hot mess of low self-esteem issues. I had recently preached a sermon about the love of God, and later that week as Stephen and I sat in the basement of a local coffee shop, he said, "Man, I wonder what my life would look like if I really believed this? How would my life be different if I was not scared, if I really believed that I am fully and totally loved by God?" Then he added, "No wonder we have liturgy and Eucharist every week. I have to hear this at least that often."

When Stephen asked, "How would my life be different if I was not scared and really believed I was loved?" I was reminded of the youth pastor's similar, yet completely different question. One question had to do with trusting God's love; the other had to do with trying to become worthy of God's love.

There is a reason Mary is everywhere. I've seen her image all over the world, in cafés in Istanbul, on students' backpacks in Scotland, in a market stall in Jakarta, but I don't think her image is everywhere because she is a reminder to be obedient, and I don't think it has to do with social revolution. Images of Mary remind us of God's favor. Mary is what it looks like to believe that we already are who God says we are.

8

The Slaughter of the Holy Innocents of Sandy Hook Elementary

Then, opening their treasure chests, they offered him gifts of gold, frankincense, and myrrh. And having been warned in a dream not to return to Herod, they left for their own country by another road. . . .

When Herod saw that he had been tricked by the wise men, he was infuriated, and he sent and killed all the children in and around Bethlehem who were two years old or under, according to the time that he had learned from the wise men.

— MATTHEW 2:11–12, 16

The week of Christmas 2012, I had tried to stick to the plan, which dictated that on the first Sunday of Christmastide we celebrate what's called "The Service of Lessons and Carols" (in which there is no sermon), or, what I like to call "The Pastor's Post–Christmas Day Break." Many of our regulars are either out of town or just really tired of church after the hullabaloo of Advent and Christmas and so, on the Sunday after Christmas day, we sing carols and read lessons and I don't have to preach and my congregation doesn't have to listen to me. It's a great plan. Unless, that is, a bunch of kids are killed in their elementary school in Newtown, Connecticut, eleven days before Christmas, and nobody knows what to think or what to do or what to say, and so they come to church hoping to at least know how to pray. In a time like that, despite a preacher's need to take some time off, that preacher's gotta preach.

So as we gathered in what felt like a solemn mass at Christmastide, I ranted a bit, telling the parishioners a story about how one of the parishes my husband, Matthew, served put on a living nativity each Advent. Members of the congregation would take turns dressing as Mary, Joseph, shepherds, and angels and would create a little manger scene in the church's parking lot where locals could drive by and see live animals hanging out near a feeding trough filled with a baby doll. It was usually pretty cold in December in Colorado, so the shifts lasted only twenty minutes before another Mary or Joseph would step in to replace the previous ones, bracing themselves against the wind and chill. One year I was helping volunteers get dressed for their nativity shifts when a seven-year-old boy came in from his twenty minutes in costume. I asked him how he had liked being a shepherd in the nativity scene.

"It was okay," he answered, "but next year I think I wanna be a pirate." You know, the pirate who was at the birth of our Lord.

Which, of course, is absurd, but is a pirate any more absurd than a drummer boy? I've given birth to two children, and in a much more comfortable setting than a barn, so I can say with certainty that the very last thing Mary wanted in her labor and delivery room was a boy playing a drum. Even if he *was* playing his "best" for her. *Get the kid with the fucking drum out of here before I hurt someone.*

A drummer boy at the birth of Jesus is the perfect example of what my friend Debbie Blue calls weird things creeping into Nativity scenes.[7] Like when, along with the sheep and goats, you occasionally see a pig in a crèche scene, as if there were swine at the birth of our Jewish Lord. Or those nativities that include a pious little Santa Claus kneeling at the manger. It all makes me want to convert to something less crazy, like Branch Davidianism.

I find myself getting pretty snotty about ridiculous commercial versions of Christmas that have no basis in the biblical text. So in the midst of trying to understand what there was for a preacher to say about children being slaughtered in their schoolrooms at Christmastime, I found myself agitated by the sentimental Christmas music, still playing in shops, and asked myself, how did Christmas go from what it was originally—a story of alienation, political tyranny, homelessness, working-class people, pagans, and angels—to a Hallmark Channel, Precious Moments, Norman Rockwell delusion? I didn't know the answer, but I suspected that certain songs were, at least in part, to blame. And hating Christmas songs is, like, what I minored in at college, so I just railed against that in the sermon since I had no idea what to say about the rest.

If I asked one hundred people the question, *who* brought gifts to the Christ child, *how many* people were there, where were the people *from,* and *where* did they bring their gifts *to* . . . inevitably everyone would respond, "Well, three kings from the Orient brought the baby Jesus gifts in the manger." And the people around would likely nod

---

7. Debbie Blue, *Sensual Orthodoxy* (Saint Paul, MN: Cathedral Hill Press, 2003).

their heads and say, "Yep, that sounds right." Three kings from the Orient bringing gifts to Jesus in a manger is a charming story, but it's not actually the one we find in the Bible.

A closer reading of Matthew shows that we have no idea how many people were there, and we don't know how far east they came from. Was it the Orient? Was it New Jersey? When they found the child, they entered not a stable or a barn with a manger but a house. And most importantly, they were definitely not kings. They were Magi, as in magicians, and not the cute kind you hire for your kid's birthday party. More likely, they were opportunistic, pagan, soothsaying, tarot-card-reading astrologers. Yet history made them out to be kings, maybe because the reality that they were magicians is too distasteful, since no one really wants the weird fortune-teller lady from the circus with her scarves and crystal balls to be the first to discover the birth of our Lord.

So the story has been niced up into an idealized picture of multicultural diplomacy. This is ironic, turning the Magi into kings, like we are doing them some great favor, because honestly everything in Matthew's story of the birth of Jesus is decidedly anti-king. I mean, there *is* a king in that text, but it's Herod: a scheming, frightened, insecure troglodyte who puts a hit out on a toddler. That is what this text has to say about kings. Turning the Magi into kings in our Christmas songs sharply represents our need to tidy up the story.

But the Epiphany story of Herod and infanticide reveals a God who has entered our world as it *actually* exists, and not as the world we often wish it would be. God's love is too pure to enter into a world that does not exist, even though this is often how we treat Jesus, like we are trying to shelter him from reality. We often behave as though Jesus is only interested in saving and loving a romanticized version of ourselves, or an idealized version of our mess of a world, and so we offer to him a

ith our Sunday school shoes on, we sing

mers at his birth, perhaps so we can escape

n the world around us.

f we use religion as the place where we es-

nstead of as the place where those difficult

t's like if you were stuck in a subway tunnel

You can respond to the fear and darkness

ng battery on your cell phone to entertain

or by using that phone as a light to see others

our of your environment, and maybe even

rce more reliable and powerful than your

to hide, numb, or even entertain ourselves

h, either through the comforting blandness
and predictability of mainline Protestantism or through the temporary
lifting of our spirits and hands in Evangelical worship. Of course, there
are many ways of pretending shit ain't broke in ourselves and in the
world, but escapist religion is a classic option, and churches have seemed
to turn into places where we have endless opportunities to pretend
everything is fine.

But church was never meant to be a place for escapism. It can and
should be a place where we dive right into difficult truths. After all, we
live in a world where in 2012, eleven days before Christmas, Adam
Lanza walked into Sandy Hook Elementary School and slaughtered
innocent children. In the middle of what was supposed to be the
"Christmas season," drummer boys and blinking lights and cheerful
music suddenly felt out of place. Instead of being in a cozy "Christmas
mood," we were left wondering, "Where the hell is God?"

When we find ourselves in a world where we see up-to-the-minute
images of human suffering like parents running past the police tape

outside an elementary school, their faces filled with primal panic not knowing if their child is alive or shot dead, can we really afford quite so much sentimentality in Christianity? Maybe soft-focus photos of doves flying in front of waterfalls, inspirational verses on coffee cups, and over-produced recordings of earnest praise music aren't really helping us. I often wonder how Jesus responds to our ignoring of reality in favor of emotional idealism, but I know for sure that the church and those we might serve aren't benefiting from it. Not when we live in a world where suffering is as real as Herod and Boko Haram and Sandy Hook, where people are longing for something to help make sense of their suffering. Pretending that everything is fine isn't helping anyone.

I love the Christmas season. I'm thrilled when we finally put up the lights and dig out the Ella Fitzgerald Christmas album (there's no "Drummer Boy" on the track list) and spend more time with family, but the story of Jesus's birth has more to offer us than that. I am not suggesting that Herod now be placed on wrapping paper or that we sit solemnly instead of joyfully in front of our roaring Christmas fire-places, but I *do* think that having the Slaughter of the Innocents take up space with singing angels and shepherds in our churches might help us know where to turn when a horrible young man kills a bunch of kids as they sit in their schoolroom. Images of Santa kneeling at a manger are comforting, maybe, but they're not helping us make sense of the world as it actually exists. The story of Christmas is as much about comfort and joy as it is about how messed up our world actually is.

The risk we run if we do not know the real Christmas story is that we can start to think that Christianity in general offers only warm sugar cookies and hot cocoa and heavenly peace as we witness children slaughtered in their schoolrooms. What is precarious about biblical il-literacy, or neglect, surrounding the Christmas story is not that we unblinkingly place shepherds and Magi together at the birth of Jesus (characters from two totally different narratives, spaced apart by years); it's that we don't think to place Herod there.

We may be used to hearing some Christians say "let's keep Christ in Christmas," but my friend Joy Carroll Wallis wrote an essay called "Keeping Herod in Christmas," and I have to say I'm with her, because the world into which Christ was born was certainly not a Norman Rockwell painting. The world has never been that world. God did not enter the world of our nostalgic, silent-night, snow-blanketed, peace-on-earth, suspended reality of Christmas. God slipped into the vulnerability of skin and entered our violent and disturbing world. *This* Christmas story, the story of Herod, the story of the Slaughter of the Holy Innocents, is as much a part of Christmas and Epiphany as are shepherds and angels.

So, on the Saturday before we gathered to hear the nine lessons traditionally read for the Service of Lessons and Carols, I told Alex, my new intern, "We're adding a reading tonight: the Slaughter of the Innocents." If someone had told me before Alex arrived at House for All that a young gay man with "the spiritual gift of joy" would be interning under me, I'd have quickly asked for a replacement. But Alex has an amazing ability to make me laugh when I get too rant-y and intense, and I love him for it. He also really, actually believes in Jesus—a big plus in my book.

"During the prayers of the people," I told him, "let's read the names of the twenty-six teachers and children who died, and maybe their ages too. We'll ring a bell after each." I had just come up with the plan and wanted to know what he thought.

"You mean twenty-seven?" he replied.

"I'm sorry, what's that?" I asked.

"Adam Lanza. The shooter. He died too."

"No way," I said before even thinking about it.

"Um, Nadia?"

Alex didn't have to say anything else. I knew he was right.

The other aspect of the story of Jesus's birth is that, as John's gospel says, a light shines in the darkness, and the darkness cannot overcome it. God chose to enter a time as violent and faithless as our own, yes. But the other thing we must confess is that the light of Christ cannot, will not, shall not ever be overcome by that darkness. Not by Herod, and not by Adam Lanza. The light of Christ is so bright that it shines even for me and even for them. (Still, Alex was a little bit of an asshole for making me face the truth of myself and the truth of God's love rather than just making me laugh, which I really would have preferred, thank you very much.)

I finally relented. "Fine," I said, "but I am registering my opposition to God's grace."

"I'm sure God is super hurt about it," Alex replied. That's better.

Two days later, when we stood in front of the congregation, Alex solemnly struck a bell for each of the names of dead teachers and children. Names illuminated, as those of the saints, Cesar Chavez's and Alma White's had been, by the light of our imperfect paschal candle.

"Charlotte Bacon, six." A bell rang.

"Daniel Barden, seven." Another bell.

"Olivia Engel, six." The vibration from each bell felt as though it were shaking my insides so hard that images of every six-year-old I'd ever known filled my mind and with each bell strike I saw them lying on a classroom floor.

I couldn't read the final name right away because it took me a minute to reach deep enough into my theological convictions in order to find the mercy to do so. I had been so intensely focused on telling the truth about the kind of world God entered and how it was as violent and faithless as our own that I had forgotten in my sermon to actually mention *why* God entered it.

If I couldn't also speak the truth that God came to save *us,* all of us, that God created us in God's image and that lives we'd rather extinguish are still precious to their maker and that the North Star that so brightly lit the way for the Magi to find the Christ child shone for them and Herod and me and Charlotte Bacon and Adam Lanza, then I really had no business being a preacher that day. So I dug deep to speak the truth of God.

"And in obedience to your command to love the enemy and pray for those who persecute us"—my voice cracked as if the courage were draining out of it—"Adam Lanza, twenty."

The final bell rang.

It is indeed right, our duty and our joy,
   that with full devotion of heart and mind and voice
   we should praise the invisible God, and the only
   Son, Jesus Christ our Lord;
who, by his precious blood, redeemed us from bondage
   to the ancient sin.
For this indeed is the Paschal Feast in which the true
   Lamb is slain,
by whose blood the doorposts of the faithful are made
   holy.

9

Frances

When he had stepped out of the boat, immediately a man out of the tombs with an unclean spirit met him. He lived among the tombs; and no one could restrain him any more, even with a chain; for he had often been restrained with shackles and chains, but the chains he wrenched apart, and the shackles he broke in pieces; and no one had the strength to subdue him. Night and day among the tombs and on the mountains he was always howling and bruising himself with stones. When he saw Jesus from a distance, he ran and bowed down before him; and he shouted at the top of his voice, "What have you to do with me, Jesus, Son of the Most High God? I adjure you by God, do not torment me." For he had said to him, "Come out of the man, you unclean spirit!" Then Jesus asked him, "What is your name?" He replied, "My name is Legion; for we are many." He begged him earnestly not to send them out of the country. Now there on the hillside a great herd of swine was feeding; and the unclean spirits begged him, "Send us into the swine; let us enter them." So he gave them permission. And the unclean spirits came out and entered the swine; and the herd, numbering about two thousand, rushed down the steep bank into the sea, and were drowned in the sea. The swineherds ran off and told it in the city and in the country. Then people came to see what it was that had happened. They

came to Jesus and saw the demoniac sitting there, clothed and in
his right mind, the very man who had had the legion; and they
were afraid. Those who had seen what had happened to the demoniac and to the swine reported it. Then they began to beg
Jesus to leave their neighborhood.

— MARK 5:2–17

My United Church of Christ pastor friend, Heather, posted this
question on my Facebook wall the week that the gospel text
was that awesomely weird story of Jesus casting a legion of
demons *out* of a naked dude and *into* a herd of pigs, pigs who
then threw themselves over a cliff and drowned in a lake:

Dear Pastor Nadia, how can I get on board with Jesus when so
much pork was wasted in the lake?
—Signed, a bacon-loving Christian

Heather is one of my best friends, even though she manages to wear
heels and look stylish while being a clergy woman *and* a mom of two
toddlers. She makes me laugh and she cares for my heart and I love her.
I posted this response:

Dear bacon-loving Christian, I guess this means the demon-
possessed-pigs-diving-off-a-cliff-and-drowning-in-a-lake story is
one that vegans and bacon lovers can unite around?

I don't always know what to do with texts about demons in the Bible. Especially when those demons talk and have names. I often wonder if, back in biblical times, people had things like epilepsy or mental illness but they didn't have the explanations provided by modern medicine and psychology like we do, so they just called it all "demon possession." Or if maybe there really were demons possessing people back then but, like polio and small pox, they were eradicated in modern times so it's just not something we have around anymore. Or perhaps we *do* actually still have demons today and we just find it more comfortable to use medical and scientific terms to describe the things that possess us. I honestly don't know.

But I do know that, like myself, many of my parishioners suffer from addictions and compulsions and depression. I do know that sometimes things get ahold of us, making us do things we don't want to or making us think we love things (substances, people, etc.) that are really destructive. So maybe if, in part, that is what having a demon is, maybe if it's being taken over by something destructive, then possession really is less of an anachronism and more of an epidemic. But thinking that those destructive things that possess us can actually talk and have first names? That's just fucked up.

As I wrote in *Pastrix,* I, like any good middle-class, mainline Protestant, tend to arrogantly look down my theological nose at talk of demon possession as superstitious snake handling nonsense, as though it's the embarrassing spiritual equivalent of a monster truck rally. My resistance to the idea that demons exist was really working for me the week we read the pork in the lake text. I was feeling squirmy about people who talk of evil spirits and demons like they are beings in and of themselves, until I remembered that, at one point in my life, my own depression had felt so present, so much like a character in my life, that it had actually felt right to go ahead and give her a name. I named my depression Frances because she moved in with me around the same time as the birth of Frances Bean, the daughter of Courtney Love and Kurt Cobain. But I picture *my* Frances as Courtney Love herself: emaciated in her torn vintage nightgown and smeared lipstick.

Frances first stopped by in my teens and early twenties and was written off by my family as me being "moody." But later, when I found myself coming to like the same things Frances liked—booze, emotionally unstable boyfriends, self-destruction—she finally just moved in, turning my studio apartment into a Wilderness.

She was a terrible roommate. She kept the place filthy and always told me devastating things about myself. When Frances lived with me, I was no longer able to do simple things, like remembering if I'd showered or shopping for groceries. I'd stand far too long looking at the dairy case, unable to make a decision about yogurt, and twenty minutes later would just leave the store empty-handed and hungry. Frances distracted me so much that I would forget to eat. Four or five months later, when my pants had gone down a couple of sizes, my parents started to worry. One day my mother, Peggy, realized that Frances was my problem and suggested I go talk to a nice lady therapist about evicting her.

She's a bit of a dope fiend, Frances, but it ends up there *is* one drug that she doesn't like. It's called Wellbutrin. Two weeks after my therapist prescribed it, the bitch was gone.

But not for good. Now, twenty years later, she still knows how to find me and sometimes shows up unannounced and stays a couple of days, even though I'm now into so many things she hates: sobriety, exercise, community, eating well, and of course, Jesus. So given my history with Frances, maybe demons having their own names and saying things out loud to Jesus is not so foreign to me after all.

When the raving demon-possessed man in Mark met Jesus at the boat, his demons were scared, and it was his demons and not the man who spoke up, saying, "What have you to do with me, Jesus, Son of the Most High God?"

It's weird, but of all the characters in the Gospels who encounter Jesus, the ones who most reliably know who he is are not the religious authorities or even Jesus's own disciples. They are the demons. The demons always recognize Jesus's authority. And the demons are afraid.

So I started wondering: If Jesus rowed up in his boat while I was in the throes of another roommate situation with my demon Frances, and I were to say to him, "What have you to do with me, Jesus, Son of the Most High God?" would Jesus say, "Oh, me? I have nothing to do with you"? Of course not. That's why the demons are afraid. Because Jesus always has something to do with them.

Which is exactly why our demons try to keep us from people who remind us how loved we are. Our demons want nothing to do with the love of God in Christ Jesus because it threatens to obliterate them, and so they try to isolate us and tell us that we are not worthy to be called children of God. And those are lies that Jesus does not abide.

Maybe my demon of anger knows to steer clear of the gospel, lest I end up forgiving some jackass who I really want to punch in the throat. Maybe your demon of inertia knows to avoid Jesus, lest it be cast off a cliff and you have to start showing up in life. Maybe your demon of compulsive eating knows to not listen to Jesus's word of love, lest it find itself drowned in a lake and you clothed and fully in your body, sitting at Jesus's feet. Maybe my demon of always, always, always having to prove myself fears Jesus since if I were to listen to Jesus and not that demon, I may start really believing that I am already good enough and then I'd have to stop overfunctioning.

The description of the Gerasene demoniac was one of someone who was completely isolated, who was out of control and alone and in pain. And if being out of control and alone and in pain was what the demon wanted, then it makes complete sense that the demon feared Jesus. Because in these healing texts, Jesus does not just cure people's diseases and cast out their demons and then say, "Mission accomplished." He's always after something more than that because the healing is never fully accomplished until there is a restoration to community. People are healed of disease, and then he tells the folks just standing around watching to go get them something to eat. The widow's son is raised from the dead and then he gives him back to his mother. And here the man healed of demons is then told to stay with his people and speak of what God has done. In the Jesus business, community is always a part of healing. Even though community is never perfect.

When the townspeople saw that the man no longer had demons and was clothed and in his right mind and sitting at Jesus's feet, they did not exactly celebrate this. Instead, they became possessed by their own demon. The text tells us that seeing this, they were seized with fear and begged Jesus to leave their town. You've seen that kind of thing before, haven't you? Like family becoming distant when you suddenly stopped hating yourself, or how your friends stopped calling when you sobered up, or how I began to resent a friend who suddenly refused to gossip with me anymore.

So are demons forces that are totally external to us who seek to defy God? Are they just the shadow side of our own souls? Are they social constructions from a premodern era? Bottom line: Who cares? I don't think demons are something human reason can put its finger on. Or that human faith can resolve. I just know that demons, whether they be addictions or actual evil spirits, are not what Jesus wants for us, since basically every time he encounters them he tells them to piss off.

The authority to face the things that lie to us, to face the things that keep us shackled, to face the things that keep us out of control, alone, and in pain and tell them in the name of Jesus to piss off is an authority that has been given to us all.

Even babies.

It was past time for the second liturgy to start at House for All, and I stood scanning the busy room, not even sure what I was looking for, when I spotted Melissa; then I knew it had to be her. After I caught her eye and motioned for her, she rose from her chair, belly first, back arched, arms pushing off the chair, supporting the weight of her pregnant body. She performed this rising with the kind of grace I'd never managed when I was pregnant. I thought of when I was that far along and Matthew and I had been in Costco and the canned clam chowder soup sample lady had asked, "You fellas wanna try some soup?" See, I didn't even manage to look pregnant. I just looked like a fat man. This memory would normally have made me smile, but not this time. Not today, not when I was this far gone with anger.

"Honey, can I borrow you for a minute?" I said to Melissa when she walked up. She agreed, and we walked to the hallway. Curiosity shone through her gorgeous brown eyes as she rubbed her huge belly and asked what was up.

There was no more hiding. "Honestly, I'm way too angry right now to start the liturgy," I said. "Would you be willing to pray for me?"

It's an inelegant thing to be a clergy person with an anger problem. I was fine during the first liturgy, but between then and now, we'd had a short congregational meeting, during which something was said that pissed the hell out of me. By an act of God, I'd dealt with it calmly and even graciously in the moment, and I had managed to not verbally eviscerate the offending parishioner during our congregational meeting. But what I could not manage was my body. I cannot control whatever chemicals course through my body in these moments.

I can go from zero to batshit crazy in no time at all. It's like a speed ball of adrenaline, cortisol, and sin—an anger accelerant—racing through my bloodstream, causing my chest and neck to tighten and my brain to shut down into single-thought mode. It makes me understand why exorcisms in the Bible were always so physical in nature. These things that take me over never seem isolated to my mind or heart (as guilty as those two are). The anger is also very physical. And you just can't lead a warm and welcoming liturgy with jaw clenched.

It reminds me of the boy who was brought to Jesus with a spirit that made him unable to speak. Whenever it seized him, it dashed him to the ground, where he foamed and ground his teeth and became rigid (Mark 9:17–18); a fair description of me when someone pisses me off.

The disciples couldn't manage to heal this boy, cast out his demon, but Jesus could. When they asked why Jesus succeeded where they'd failed (an eternally stupid question), he said, "This kind [of demon] can come out only through prayer" (verse 29).

Same with mine. Except that night my demon came out through prayer...and babies.

Melissa and I stood in that hallway as she took in the information— without pause or judgment—that her pastor was too angry to do her job. She moved her hands from her belly and offered them for me to hold.

It sounds crazy now, to say that I particularly needed a pregnant woman to pray for me. But I did. I needed someone with innocent life in her flesh to pray out the demon in mine because sometimes only beauty can release ugliness.

But I also knew it couldn't be just any pregnant lady. It had to be this one. This twenty-six-year-old social worker who counsels survivors of sexual assault. I needed this woman who glides as though on invisible wheels, who is propelled by a fierce, determined, and practiced belief in loving-kindness that can come only from seeing its power in the face of evil. She looked at me through her brown bangs and did not say, "Oh Nadia, I'm so sorry you are having a hard day, what happened?" No. She simply took my hands and commended me to her Lord.

"God, Nadia's in a bad place and we need her back. Your people need their pastor. Break her heart with our love for her and release what binds her."

As she prayed, some of the horribleness left me, enough at least to get church started.

During open space, the ten-minute period of prayer and reflection that follows the sermon, I spotted a family who I'd seen carrying their five-week-old twins into church. I walked up, my arms extended toward one of the babies like it was Aquafina in the Mojave.

"Would you mind?" I asked.

"Of course not," the father said.

Holding the tiny baby in my arms, I could swear my brain was immediately awash in oxytocin. Like a baptism of neurochemicals that did for me what self-talk and even prayer could not fully accomplish. I held that child with one arm and stared at it, lost in the complete gift of it all.

Perhaps this release of neurochemicals is what people are seeking to accomplish through those cute pictures of babies and puppies on Facebook. But, as comic Larry Miller says (of something less innocent), the difference between holding a baby and seeing a baby on Facebook is the difference between shooting a bullet and throwing a bullet.

It took a few beats before I realized that announcements had ended and everyone was looking my way, waiting for me to start the next part of the liturgy. I just wasn't ready to let go of the baby. For me, in that moment, that beautiful baby and my friend Melissa were Jesus, rowing up in the boat. "What the hell do you have to do with me?" my anger asked. And at their touch, all the toxins left my body and were cast away. Perhaps into suicidal swine somewhere in Colorado, who knows, but I was free.

I motioned to her father. "Can I hold her awhile longer?"

He nodded, and I proceeded to preside at the table with one arm free and one rocking an infant. With what felt like an entirely changed brain chemistry, I rocked as I chanted.

It is indeed right, our duty and our joy that we should at all times and in all places offer thanks and praise to you . . .

Later, I described this experience as "the baby of life, the holding of which is for the healing of the people." Because the holy things we need for healing and sustenance are almost always the same as the ordinary things right in front of us.

10

Panic Attack in Jericho

By the time we got to the Monastery of the Temptation above Jericho, I had already asked all twenty of the people in my tour group if anyone had Valium. Sure, it's a controlled substance and I'm in recovery, but at the time, it felt like my only hope, as if I were a Princess Leia hologram projected out of a droid and antianxiety medication was Obi-Wan.

My fellow tourists had just spent an hour watching the landscape outside our bus windows turn from brown to green as we entered the Valley of Fire. But I had spent the hour unable to focus on anything but my total mortal fear of driving on mountain roads. Who cares what the scenery looks like when your imminent-death-by-falling-off-a-cliff-in-a-bus is so clearly just moments away from happening? We had just driven our tour bus down a steep one-lane—but with two-way traffic— road (which would never be legal in the States) that boasted too few guardrails but enough hairpin turns to keep me praying and cursing, praying and cursing, like a monk with Tourette's.[8]

---

8. There *is* a perfectly safe, well-lit Israeli road that goes from Bethlehem to Jericho, but our tour guide, a Palestinian Lutheran named Hassam, was, like Jesus himself, born in Bethlehem (and resides there) and therefore had the wrong color ID card to be allowed to travel on the safe road.

I'd gone on this two-week-long trip to the Holy Land hoping to see some of the places Jesus had been, but I didn't anticipate calling on him in prayer quite so much on a single bus ride near his place of birth.

The terrifying road we'd taken to get to Jericho from Bethlehem in the West Bank was the same road we'd be taking home, and given how I'd almost lost my mind on the way down, I knew the only way I would make it back up was to be drugged or perhaps knocked unconscious. So I made my way person to person in my group, trying to see if anyone had something I could take for anxiety. Also, I was trying to do this without making myself seem too pathetic. No dice. Apparently, no one else but me in my group had anxiety issues, so the odds of me not seeming pathetic were pretty slim.

For many of the twenty people on my Holy Land tour, all really nice Lutheran folks from the Midwest, this would be the first time I had really spoken to them. I'd been keeping my distance since I joined the trip four days before and thought it best to keep it that way. I had managed to meet other people everywhere we went, making nice with those visiting the same religious sites or eating in the same cafés. I was friendly enough to strangers I knew I'd be interacting with for only a few moments, but I was too afraid to risk connecting with anyone in my own tour group. You have to pay attention to people if you want to connect with them, and I worried that if I paid too much attention, I might make the realization that I didn't like them. If that happened, I'd have to spend all my energy *pretending* I liked them, and I'd have no energy left to avoid looking out the window at my terrifying bird's-eye view of the Holy Land.

I tend to maintain a similar policy on airplanes (unless, of course, the person next to me has pink bangs and a snide little message from the Almighty). Usually I hide in magazines and headphones until the final descent, when I will finally choose to be friendly to the person in the next seat. "So, are you coming home or leaving home?" That way, even if he or she is annoying or—worse—boring, the conversation will last ten minutes, tops. So it was four days into the tour and I was stuck having made no real connection to anyone.

A month earlier and in a panic, I had called Bishop Bruce, the tour guide for this trip to Israel and Palestine and also the friend I'd made at the ELCA assembly. He and his recently deceased wife, Cynthia, had led this trip together for over a decade, and this was the first year he would be doing it alone. Since I had supported him while Cynthia was dying, he was pleased I was interested in possibly coming.

"Bruce, how do I say this . . . I'm worried about the trip."

Bruce began to walk me through what it's like to go through Israeli checkpoints, and he assured me that the West Bank is perfectly safe.

I cut him off. "Sorry, that's not what I meant. I meant being with a group of Midwesterners in a tour bus for two weeks. My breathing is getting irregular just thinking about it." I felt out of control at the thought of being stuck for two weeks with people who might want something from me, like to laugh at their puns or look at photos of their grandchildren.

"Nadia, if you are trying to get me to say that no one on this trip will annoy you, I'm afraid you are putting me in the weird position of having to lie." Bruce wasn't one to coddle. He said that if I needed space, I could opt out of an event or two, and so I had considered skipping this day trip from Bethlehem to Jericho but knew I'd regret not seeing the mountain Monastery of the Temptation and the gondola ride over Jericho, humanity's oldest known home. So I went. But no one told me about the fucking road. Perhaps I should have let Bruce finish telling me what is dangerous about the West Bank because, given the opportunity, surely he would have mentioned the road.

When we finally arrived in Jericho and were in line for the gondola that would take us up to the cliff-dwelling monastery, I made my way up the queue asking for drugs, trying to nonchalantly explain that I have a little phobia that I wasn't sure I could face twice in one day.

"Sharon, do you have any Valium or something like it?" I was shocked I got her name right, but still, the kind-faced middle-aged midwife from Wisconsin just offered me the same sincere, tilted-head Midwestern look of concern, sigh, and "sorry" that I had received from everyone else as I made my way through the group. One by one they all seemed crestfallen that they could not help me. Asking that many people for something began to feel like it was putting a real chink in my "keeping my distance, thank you very much" armor, yet still, I'm certain the response was one of sincere concern and kindness.

When he realized how afraid I was of our return trip, Sharon's husband, Mark, a Lutheran pastor who wore khaki pants that zipped at the knees and converted into shorts, took my arm and said, "I'll help you face your phobia if you help me face mine." He nodded his head to the red gondola that had just unloaded a group of German speakers and loaded a group of folks in matching blue T-shirts from a church in Kenya. "Heights," he said with a tone usually reserved for words like *leukemia* or *zombies*.

I have no problem with heights myself, but I genuinely felt for him. Fear of things other people are fine with is just embarrassing.

We ended up in different gondolas, Mark and I, but I did say a prayer for him as mine rocked back and forth, high into the dry Palestinian sky.

As we rose in the air, more of the valley came into view—olive trees, lush vegetation, wavy hills—and it brought to mind one of the more famous prostitutes in the Bible, since she had once lived in this valley. Rahab had aided a couple of Israelite spies—she hid them when they were doing some recon for the attack Israel had been planning against them—and in return for her hospitality and help, she and her family were the only citizens of Jericho spared when the Israelites brought down the walled city.

I sat in my gondola wondering if my view was perhaps similar to what Rahab herself had seen from her home, which we are told was built into the walls of the city. What had changed in this valley since Joshua fought the Battle of Jericho? Had she seen out her window the rocks and hills and olive trees that I now saw falling below me as my gondola rose up the mountain? As we ascended, I thought of how God had sent a prostitute to help the Hebrew spies who would, through her help, and only through her help, conquer the city and fell the walls. I also wondered: Had that been humiliating to them? Receiving help from a whore? Would they rather have done it all by themselves or with help from someone of their choosing?

When our gondola arrived at the top, several folks from my tour group and I exited along with a stranger, an impeccably dressed older German woman in a Gucci scarf—traveling alone—who was having difficulty finding her balance.

"Would you like to walk together?" I asked, offering my arm and nodding my head toward the steep five-hundred-meter stone walk that led to the entrance of the monastery. She and I spent the next hour together walking through, praying, and sharing in the wonder of those ancient buildings hewn out of the side of a cliff by Byzantine Christians in the sixth century who wanted to escape the world around them. I wondered how long it took for those original inhabitants and those who followed, who also wanted nothing more than to be left alone, to realize that they took all the problems of society with them in small, even cellular, ways, within themselves. I wondered if they had that "wherever you go, there you are" feeling at the moment they realized that there really is nowhere you can hide from human bullshit, since we just bring it with us wherever we go.

Having successfully avoided my own tour group at the mountain monastery, I found myself on the return trip down the mountain in a gondola filled not with Midwesterners but with five Kenyans—their rich dark skin contrasting with the cheerful turquoise T-shirts they wore. I took my seat, and when our gondola began moving, the large, beautiful woman next to me grabbed my knee with her shaking hand as she fought to breathe.

Her friend, who was sitting across from us, saw my slightly stunned expression. "She's afraid," he said.

Without thinking, I placed my left hand on the shaking hand of this terrified stranger, and with my right hand I rubbed her back.

"You're okay. I am right here," I said. And, after just experiencing over an hour of reflection about our surroundings, I continued, "If God can bring down the walls of Jericho, God can get this gondola down safely. You are okay. I am right here." Her friends started singing hymns and I kept praying.

She kept her head down and her hand on my knee and I had no idea if she even spoke English and understood what I was saying, but I just kept saying it. Perhaps she never would have chosen a tattooed American lady to be the one to meet her need, to be present to her fear and to pray as she fought to breathe. But the spies never thought Rahab, a prostitute of all people, would be the one to help them either. Sometimes help comes from unexpected places.

At the bottom, the rest of my group, which was assembled and waiting for me, witnessed the five Kenyans and I hug each other upon exiting the gondola. My Kenyan sister whose name I will never know finally released my hand and raised her arms to heaven saying, "Praise Jesus." We had gotten down the mountain together. But now I had to face getting back up the other side on that road without antianxiety meds and without losing my composure and crushing someone's knee with my own shaking hand.

Once, years ago, a group of my friends and I were sitting around the lobby of a hotel, having escaped from a pointless clergy meeting in a conference hall. Someone suggested we all go around and say out loud the adjective that, if someone used it to describe us, would be the absolute worst. "Boring," someone confessed; "failure" from another. When it got to me there was no equivocating. I shifted around in the overly colorful hotel armchair before finally saying, "Needy."

My mother claims that the first time I said more than one word at a time, I skipped the two-word combinations altogether and went right to "Do it self." Yes, thank you very much, I will do it myself. I do not want to need anyone else. After years of therapy and twelve-step work, I've finally realized that trying not to need others isn't about strength and independence; it's about fear. To allow myself to need someone else is to put myself in a position to be betrayed or made to look weak. Not that this realization ever really helps me in the moment. I want to "do it self." I want to make my own decisions and not be beholden to a tour group, and I want everyone to understand that I am strong as hell, which is increasingly difficult to pull off when you've just asked everyone if they have Valium and they don't and they know how scared you are of the stupid fucking unlit road you are now about to go up *in the dark*.

Evening had fallen, and when we boarded the tour bus, I walked down the aisle attempting to figure out which seat would best allow me to ignore the road, but that would take talking to someone, so I chose a right-hand seat in front of Susan, a woman in her fifties from Madison, Wisconsin, who had a touch of smartassness to her and who had made me laugh earlier in the day when, at lunch, she cracked wise about having to "eat hummus again!" I thought that if I turned around and engaged her in conversation, I could be distracted enough to not completely lose it on the drive.

"Susan, do you think we might get to indulge in a little hummus at dinner when we get back?" I offered sarcastically, after the bus had been on the road for a few moments.

"Only if we are really—" She was cut off by a crunching sound under the bus that caused us all to jump. I had been doing fine. Really, I was totally cool. I wasn't looking out the windows. I was trying to joke around with the lady behind me, until it sounded like the bus ran over something, or hit an animal—I couldn't tell. I snapped my head around and saw nothing out my window but the side face of the cliff.

We hadn't hit anything. But the bus had failed to successfully make a hairpin turn, and half a second before my head registered what had happened enough for the "panic now" chemicals to wash over my brain, Susan put her hand on my shoulder. She knew this was not going to be good.

Our bus was straddling both sides of a hairpin turn; the left side of the bus hovered over a cliff and the right side of the bus blocked traffic in both directions. Our driver tried and failed to move the bus forward, and as the clutch engaged, the bus lurched back a couple of feet.

"Get out!" the bus driver shouted, opening the door on the right side of the bus, the side that was still attached to the road. "Leave your things and get out!"

I escaped from that forty-person coffin with everyone else and found a large slab of concrete next to the road on which to grab my knees and lose my shit. It was as though I could no longer pull oxygen into my lungs—the air couldn't get past my throat before being exhaled like a rejection. Over and over. I had lost the ability to control my breathing or my thoughts or my shaking hands. My knees were soaked in my own tears.

I don't remember Sharon, the midwife, approaching me, but her hands had just suddenly landed on top of mine. "You are okay. I am here." Then she placed her hands on my shoulders and spoke warmly to me. Were her hands not there, something would have escaped from me—like my sanity, or my ability to have my consciousness and body together in one place. She was holding the lid on for me.

Eventually, the driver righted the bus via a series of back and forth maneuvers, and it came time for my group to reboard.

"I'm not getting on that bus. I'm not getting on that bus," I kept repeating to Sharon.

Sharon told Bishop Bruce on my behalf that I was, under no circumstances, to get on the bus. She was so strong and grounded and everything I was not in that moment and I needed her more than I needed anything else. And yet, an hour earlier, like a complete asshole, I had a hard time remembering her name.

Bruce hailed the first car that drove by. The windows of an Audi rolled down and from the driver came the greeting "Father! We have not seen you for a while."

This from a slightly balding, middle-aged, cigarette-brandishing Palestinian on a random road in the West Bank. To be fair, everyone in the West Bank seemed to know Bruce and call him Father, but this felt like a miracle nonetheless.

Bruce explained the situation, and the driver agreed to take me—the crying, shaking, crazy American woman—the rest of the way up the road and into Bethlehem.

He flung his cigarette out the window and said, "Welcome." They all say welcome in that land.

The next morning, I was the first to arrive at breakfast. The room was bright with the morning sun, and the newness of the light felt like hope to me. Like that cleared-out feeling you get after a really good cry, or a really embarrassing panic attack in front of twenty people from Wisconsin.

I sat at a table alone until some of the members of my tour group—Susan, Sharon, and her husband, Mark, the Lutheran pastor—gathered with their coffee and their Middle Eastern breakfasts of hummus and pita and hard-boiled eggs. As I motioned for them to join me, I realized that the humiliation of the previous evening had almost faded, and in its place I felt an open-hearted fondness for them. A gratitude. In my rawest, most unguarded state, they had seen me completely lose control of my mind and my sinuses and they didn't make a big deal of it. They just wanted to make sure I was okay.

Whatever I had been trying to protect had been taken from me on that road. I had become *needy* and unable to "do it self" and yet I had survived. I received help from those I was trying to avoid, and I had survived. It was like a spiritual exfoliation by humiliation.

My heart had opened. Maybe not so much that I would laugh at corny puns, but when Sharon and Mark laid their plates down next to mine and took their seats, I asked, "So, Sharon, do you guys have grandkids?"

This is the night
in which, in ancient times, you delivered our forebears,
the children of Israel, and led them, dry-shod, through
the sea.

This is the night
in which the darkness of sin has been purged away by the
rising brightness.

This is the night
in which all who believe in Christ are rescued from evil
and the gloom of sin, are renewed in grace, and are
restored to holiness.

This is the night
in which, breaking the chains of death, Christ arises from
hell in triumph.
O night truly blessed which alone was worthy to know the
time and hour in which Christ arose again from hell!

This is the night
of which it is written: "The night is as clear as the day," and,
"then shall my night be turned into day."
The holiness of this night puts to flight the deeds of wickedness; washes away sin; restores innocence to the fallen, and
joy to those who mourn; casts out hate; brings peace; and
humbles earthly pride.

11

Parlors

On the day before Fat Tuesday, 2014, I stood in a small restaurant on Denver's tree-lined Sixth Avenue, looking hungrily at the food set out for Billy's memorial service. The locally owned restaurant, Satchel's on 6th, had the simple, clean look of a place owned and run by foodies. I was famished, and the chocolates and flatbreads looked amazing, but no one else was eating.

It's not that uncommon—people usually don't feel hungry at a funeral; or maybe they do and think it would look bad to take advantage of free artisan cheeses when someone has just died. It's always so mismatched: the people who cook in response to grief and the people who refuse to eat in response to grief. Perhaps the platters of leftovers are their own comfort when taken home by the bereaved, like piles of sustenance for the bitter days to come. But unlike everyone else in the room, my hunger was uncurbed by grief because I'd never met Billy.

A week earlier, I had answered the phone thinking it was my doctor's office returning my call. Instead I was greeted by, "Is this Nadia?"

I groaned. Like most modern Americans, I never answer the phone if I don't recognize the number. However, just minutes before the phone rang, I had been told by my doctor's office that they would call me right back. So this time I had picked up.

"I got your number from Becky Kunzelman," the voice on the other end said. Yeah, not my doctor. Becky is a world-renowned Cross-Fit athlete and devout Christian from Denver. Turns out Becky had just read *Pastrix,* so when a woman from her gym asked if she knew a pastor who would do a funeral for her nephew, a young gay man who had hanged himself the day before, Becky called my coach, Neil, and asked for my number.

The funeral was to be the following Monday, but the following Monday was one of only three days off I would have that month, and I needed it. I'd been on the road at least once a week for weeks while pastoring House for All full-time and, frankly, I felt like I'd "given at the office." She kept talking and I kept shaking my head, thinking, *No way. No way. No way. Nope.*

"Billy was such a creative soul," the woman on the phone said. "But he was in a lot of pain. Emotional pain. He worked in the kitchen at Satchel's restaurant. That's where the funeral is, by the way, with all the kids he worked with. He was an artist, so creative, but he was tortured. Bipolar, they say, but who knows. He, um, well, he hanged himself."

The more she talked, the more I both resisted the idea and knew that I had to do it.

"Anyhow," she continued, "I understand if you can't do it, but do you know another pastor who might be right for this?"

Fuck. Everything in me was trying to protect myself, trying to preserve the little unscheduled time I had. In most cases, that's the right move. But not this time.

My congregation was pretty young, so I'd done funerals only a couple of times before, and one of those was for a good friend who had also hanged himself. PJ was creative and bipolar too, and in my initial resistance to do this funeral, it felt as though I'd almost forgotten about PJ, his funeral, and the particular pain that suicide brings to those left behind.

I said I'd need a day to think about it, but seven minutes later, I texted her. "Yes. It would be my honor to do Billy's funeral. He sounds like one of my people."

A week later, as I walked around Satchel's, I didn't touch the gorgeous food all around me. Instead, I looked at photos of Billy lovingly displayed around the room as his family, friends, and coworkers filed in. Billy seemed to have a thing for cutoff shorts and goofy smiles.

Billy's mom sat on a wooden bench along the wall while her family held her hand. I had visited her home a couple of days earlier and asked questions about her son. She had beautiful Carole King hair, and I'd even be willing to bet there was a copy of *Tapestry* somewhere in her small Victorian apartment across from City Park. Her place was filled with houseplants, vibrant colors, and gorgeous mandalas one might expect from someone like herself: a faculty member of Naropa University, a Buddhist school in Boulder. Despite her grief, there was something that kept her tethered to the ground. Billy's ex-wife was there. She had thin bird wrists and short bangs, and she was sad and suspicious. I suspected she would be the first to react dismissively if I said something stupid. Billy's sister and brother, both younger and by all accounts better adjusted, seemed both frustrated by and totally in love with their wild brother.

I listened and asked questions, and when I sensed they wanted me to say something pastor-y, I told them about my friend PJ who had committed suicide, because I wanted them to know that if love alone could have kept PJ alive, he would still be here. And how, as sacred as love is, human love is never pure or perfect. We just aren't that kind of species. There are cracks in everything and even the most shining aspects of our lives—even love, or perhaps especially love—come with imperfection.

Often, when someone dies, we feel a combination of love and something else, and this, too, is holy. And entirely human. And they don't cancel each other out. Love and anger. Love and disappointment. Love and emptiness. We always love imperfectly. It is the nature of human love. And it is okay.

But despite all the love in the world, when it comes down to it, none of us can know the reality of another. We can share circumstances, personality traits, even parents, yet as much as we move through our lives alongside each other, none of us can fully know the internal reality of another. These people sitting on those benches at Satchel's, the people who loved Billy the very most and felt they knew him the very best, might never have known the type of pain Billy was in. Or the love he knew. Or the isolation he experienced.

I know what it's like to think, in response to the suicide of someone I love, "I should have returned his last voice mail," or, "I should have checked in on him more," or, "I should have had more patience with him." But I also know that's not how it works. And after someone is lost, we are left with only what is left: our own persistent longing for things to have been different and for those we love not to have been in pain and, mostly, for them to have remained with us. I remember how angry I was at PJ, how tenderness accompanied that anger, and yet how certain I was, in the midst of my tender anger, that God could hold all of our inconsistencies, including PJ's terminal ones.

People are cynical about religion, and about Christianity especially. I know this. I sensed that cynicism in the room at Satchel's—that perhaps people were wondering why a Lutheran pastor was doing a funeral for a person, family, and group of people who were, for the most part, not Christian. And I get it. I can be cynical myself. Every time I see some smiley TV preacher talk about God's plan for me or hear Sarah Palin say something irretrievably mean and stupid about poor people, or every time I pass an embarrassing billboard featuring Jesus and a fetus, I totally get why reasonable people would keep their distance. I get why having a Christian pastor at a non-Christian memorial service for a young, gay, bipolar man who took his own life could sound like a weird, even bad, idea.

Yet I felt more at home in that room than I had a few days earlier at a Presbyterian church in Indiana, and suddenly I realized that what I had initially resisted (doing a funeral for folks who weren't my parishioners on one of my three days off that month) was actually what I desperately needed in order to be faithful to my call. These mourners still felt to me like part of my parish. And I wanted more than anything to preach about Jesus. Not in a "here's my chance to get you to believe the right things" type of way, but more in a "I get how distasteful so much of this Christianity stuff can be, but it's also just the most real and beautiful thing I have ever heard" type of way. The Jesus story connects with Billy's because it, too, is a story of love and suffering.

So I offered to this group of nonreligious parishioners a reading from the gospel of Matthew:

> For John came neither eating nor drinking, and they say, "He has a demon"; the Son of Man came eating and drinking, and they say, "Look, a glutton and a drunkard, a friend of tax collectors and sinners!" Yet wisdom is vindicated by her deeds. (11:18–19)

I've never fully understood how Christianity became quite so tame and respectable, given its origins among drunkards, prostitutes, and tax collectors. So I read this short passage and explained that I didn't know Billy but that I do know queer, and I know addiction, and I know depression. (Not to mention that, as a former restaurant worker, I also know what it's like to spill shit in the walk-in and have to clean it up in the middle of the dinner rush.)

I told them that when I heard Billy was bright, an artist and musician, and when I heard that he loved his family and loved people through difficulty in relationships, and when I heard that he struggled with heroin and booze addictions and an unhelpful brain chemistry, and when I heard that he was beautifully queer and passionate and sometimes played piano in his sister's dresses, I knew. I knew that Billy was pretty much exactly the kind of person Jesus would hang out with.

I told them that Jesus could have hung out in the high-end religious scene of his day, but instead he scoffed at all that, choosing instead to laugh at the powerful, befriend whores, kiss sinners, and eat with all the wrong people. He spent his time with people for whom life was not easy. And there, amid those who were suffering, he was the embodiment of perfect love.

I looked Billy's mother in the eyes and said that what I know for sure is that God is always present in love and in suffering. And that God was present both the moment Billy entered this world and the moment he left it, loving him back into the arms of his Creator.

She mouthed, "Thank you."

✤

What I did not know at the time was that thirty hours after standing in a restaurant for a funeral of one child, I would stand—on Ash

Wednesday—in the birthing room of another. Just a little more than a day after preaching in a bar about love and suffering and Jesus, I would hold the baby of my parishioners Duffy and Charlie in my arms and thank God for brand-new life.

God: present in love, present in rooms where women give birth, present in rooms where families wrestle with suffering and death.

What I find interesting is that death used to be more a part of life than it is for us now, and not just because we have a longer life expectancy and a lower infant mortality rate than we did two hundred years ago. Death used to be a part of life because, like birth, it was something we did at home.

Until the late nineteenth century, the front room in houses, called the parlor, was where one would receive guests, but it was also where the bodies of the dead would be laid out for visitation. People used to die at home, at which point their loved ones would wash and prepare the body and lay it in the parlor. Neighbors, friends, and family would come to see the body and perhaps stroke the hair or kiss the forehead of those who had gone to their rest. Death was a part of life. That is, until the advent of the funeral parlor, a local for-profit business that took over all that unpleasantness for us. (This is when and why the front room in our home started to be called the "living" room and not the parlor.)

We've relegated death, birth, and even making music to the professionals . . . all things that, until a few generations ago, used to be done by regular people like us in the home. What used to be *natural*— giving birth, playing instruments and singing, and dying among loved ones who will lovingly lay our bodies out in the parlor to be honored by those who loved us—is now a commercial enterprise. Not that I'm ungrateful for a lower infant mortality rate or the safety that women in high-risk pregnancies now enjoy, and not that I don't love hearing professionally recorded music. But I do wonder if we lost more than we realized when we started hiring professionals to do for us what we used to do for ourselves.

Anyway, here I was on Ash Wednesday, standing in a birthing room at the University of Colorado Hospital, on the day that the church remembers that we are but dust and to dust we will return. With one hand, I held a small metal pot of ashes and with the other, I reached across Duffy's recovery bed and made the sign of the cross with black ashes on her forehead, then on Charlie's too. Duffy had that beautiful and totally exhausted look of a woman who had just given birth, and Charlie had that proud and totally exhausted look of a partner who had just spent hours feeling helpless.

"The baby too?" I then asked her parents.

Duffy and Charlie said, "Yes, please, the baby too."

My voice strained a bit as I pressed ever so gently into the brow of baby Willa's brand-new skin, flesh that had been exposed to air for only a few precious hours. I couldn't completely constrain the trembling in my voice as I reminded all of us in the room that even she, full of beauty and hope and just hours from her mother's womb, will, at her death, return to dust and the very heart of God.

And the mother mouthed, "Thank you."

And then I knew. I knew more than on any other Ash Wednesday that the promises of baptisms and funerals, the promises of birth and death, are inextricably wrapped up together. For we come from God and to God we shall go. There is so much that gets in the way of that simple truth. And it is times like funerals and births when all the other BS just doesn't matter anymore.

Here's my image of Ash Wednesday: If our lives were a long piece of fabric with our baptism on one end and our funeral on another, and we don't know the distance between the two, then Ash Wednesday is a time when that fabric is pinched in the middle and the ends are held up so that our baptism in the past and our funeral in the future meet. The water and words from our baptism plus the earth and words from our funerals have come from the past and future to meet us in the present. And in that meeting we are reminded of the promises of God: That we are God's, that there is no sin, no darkness, and yes, no grave that God will not come to find us in and love us back to life. That where two or more are gathered, Christ is with us. These promises outlast our earthly bodies and the limits of time.

I knew as I stood in Willa's birthing room and held the tiny infant and watched with fascination as she moved her head on her tiny neck and smacked her perfect little mouth that somehow the suffering and love of Billy's mother's labor, twenty-nine years earlier, was held in the hands of God. I knew in that exquisite moment that the love and suffering of another mother's labor just today was also held in the hands of God and that she, too, must commend her child to the one from whom that child came.

Billy and Willa. Two beloved children of God whom Jesus came to save. And to claim. And to befriend. And to welcome home.

Ashes to ashes. Dust to dust.

12

The Lame

I f there were odds against Amy—that as a paraplegic she wouldn't survive childhood, that she would never be a great dancer, that she would not be a sexual being, that she could never support herself in a career, that she would never drive a red convertible sports car, that she would never live in her own home on her own terms—she unapologetically beat them. Amy was not to be messed with. She drank wine at lunch, wore too many sparkly clothes and baubles, and could roll her eyes like she had a human idiot meter hard-wired into her head.

Amy in her chair was a titanium mermaid—but not the Disney princess kind of mermaid. She was the "I'm living *big* without legs" kind. It was amazing that so much sass and sarcasm could fit inside such a tiny broken body, but it did.

Her best friend Bobbie had often said that, emotionally speaking, being around Amy was like "standing in front of a fire hose." But if Amy was a fire hose, Bobbie was a brick wall.

Bobbie has that particular brand of awkwardness that is only born out of pain. It's always below the surface, that kind of pain, tucked inside an impermeable encasing. Childhood sexual abuse does things to a developing psyche that forever change its direction. Of course what direction the growth takes is varied. Some victims become abusers themselves, inflicting what was inflicted. Some prune their own lives down to nothing, disappearing into needles, razors, carbohydrates. Some develop lives in which they have careers, family, and community, but always walk through that life with protective layers hiding away their own damage.

For Bobbie, there is always something painful right below what she says, and somehow that pain is both too surfaced to ignore and yet too buried to mention. When she talks, she laughs a lot. A nervous laugh, one that is a response not to humor but to discomfort. It's hard to know how to respond to a laugh like that and, well, it's awkward. So awkward, in fact, that for a while I had a hard time knowing how to appreciate Bobbie.

There was a point, early in the life of House for All Sinners and Saints, when I was baffled by how many socially awkward people like Bobbie were showing up. I mean, the church was tiny, maybe twenty to thirty people, and there were a few folks who were magnetic, energizing, and, you know, cool. But the "Bring Your Own Brain" Bible study that I started holding weekly in the basement of a hipster bar in Denver didn't attract those people. Why? Because compelling, dynamic people who are natural leaders are *busy*. They have a lot of demands on their time and attention. Instead, those who showed up to my Tuesday night Bible study were people who could have attended if it were Wednesday, Thursday, Friday, or Saturday. These folks had five or six nights of the week *free*.

I'd convinced myself that this church would never have a chance if these were the kinds of people who showed up. At the same time, bloggers and church pundits (who had never visited House for All) began to claim, based on the fact that the pastor was tattooed and pastors attract people like themselves, that our church was obviously just a church for hipsters. Which has never, ever been the case. Those without tattoos and ironic eyewear outnumber those who do by about thirty to one.

So eventually I started to ask myself, "Wait. Why am I not attracting other cool people? I mean, why *aren't* there people like me coming?" (Now might be a good time to ask the obvious: What kind of person thinks this shit?)

✝

Soon after they met in 2002, Bobbie, the emotional cripple, would become Sherpa to Amy, the physical cripple. From the outside, it looked as though Bobbie was selflessly and compassionately taking care of a disabled woman. She hauled Amy's crooked little body around to concerts and road trips and Scottish festivals (where reportedly, Amy was known for lifting up a kilt or two from her auspicious position in the wheelchair). And when Amy was in the ICU for weeks, intubated and barely alive, Bobbie rarely left her side in what would appear, again, simply to be an act of benevolence toward someone less fortunate than herself. And it was hard not to feel bad about my own selfish, fickle, sometimes ugly approach to loving (or *not* loving) others, especially seeing how Bobbie cared for Amy. Unwavering. Selfless. Beautiful. I admired it. But I can't say I understood it.

Bobbie was the one who found Amy Mack's body, like we always assumed would be the case. Amy's heart had given out, and having found her, Bobbie's heart had, for a while and in a different way, done the same.

By the time I arrived at Amy's condo, Bobbie Jo was sitting on the front steps in the cool spring sun waiting for the Denver medical examiner to rule out foul play as the cause of Amy's death.

I hugged Bobbie but was unsure what to say. Bobbie Jo and Amy Mack were soul sisters, best friends, and partners in crime.

"I'm sorry, honey." That was about all I could muster before the examiner came out and said we could now have some time with the body before it was taken by the coroner.

"But only a couple of minutes," he said.

When I anointed Amy, I defiantly took my time since, as I mentioned earlier, it isn't often that we get the opportunity to experience a living room as a parlor. As I traced the sign of the cross on her cool forehead, my fingers easily gliding over the oil to form the cross, I was taken back to just four days earlier, on Ash Wednesday, when I had visited Duffy and Charlie and made the same sign with ashes on the head of baby Willa, just hours old, remembering that we are God's and to God we return.

In Amy's apartment, surrounded by decorative mermaids and mementos, Bobbie Jo and I, along with another friend, Ellen, who had arrived a moment earlier, needed to honor the body of our friend. Especially *this* body. This eighty-five-pound, broken, paraplegic body. We stroked her dirty-blond hair and lightly, lovingly touched her cool face, already gone stiff from half a day without life.

"You belong to God to whom you have returned," I said and kissed her face, and then Bobbie kissed her forehead, right on the oily cross, sealing it with her love.

Later, when the coroner awkwardly lifted Amy from the wheelchair to the stretcher, Bobbie informed him, "Her legs haven't been straight for fifteen years. Don't try to make them that way now."

✢

It had been the night before Thanksgiving in 1965 when five-year-old Amy was thrown through the back window of a pick-up truck. Some-one had had too many drinks and someone else would never walk again, and tragically, that's the way that story usually goes. She hated the "fucking wheelchair," as she called it, that she was sentenced to after the accident, but never in the fifty years hence did she let it define her. (At one point a few years earlier I even asked, "Hey, Amy, is 'fucking,' like, the first name of your wheelchair?" She replied with a simple bony middle finger.)

⊹

At Amy's memorial service, Bobbie read her list of things she wanted to thank Amy for. Standing next to Bobbie Jo as she gave this little eulogy was a small shrine for her best friend: mermaids, a sparkly cloth, a photo of Amy's wheelchair parked without its occupant in a stunning mountain valley, and of course, again, our shining, imperfect paschal candle.

It took Bobbie a second at the microphone before she could begin.

Thank you, Amy.

Thank you for seeing me, for seeing through the facade, for suddenly shouting "Boudicca!" at me in the middle of poetry group.

Thanks for driving through that thunderstorm with the top down—you were right, we didn't get wet.

Thanks for praying, and for refusing to pray, and thereby becoming a living prayer.

Thanks for your honesty, for your frustration and anger and enthusiasm and joy.

Thanks for your adventurous spirit. Who else would let me haul them out into the middle of accessible-nowhere and leave them sitting on a rock far from their wheelchair—and enjoy every minute?

Thank you for your poet's heart, for the music of honest and beautiful words that turn the struggles of life into a song of shared humanity.

Thanks for the laughter and silliness and the random quoting of movie lines in restaurants (or anywhere else)—mostly from "Madagascar" or "Joe Versus the Volcano."

Thanks for seeing, really seeing, people who often get overlooked: restaurant staff who became quick friends, a panhandler asking for change, and me.

Thank you for your music and singing, for air guitar in the living room, for taking me to hear great live bands, for making me get up in front of everyone and dance with you until I got dizzy from spinning.

Thank you for nudging me—okay, pushing me, yanking me sometimes kicking and screaming—outside of my comfort zone.

Thanks for sharing candidly your unique view of life, the universe, and everything—and saying out loud what other people are thinking but are too inhibited to express.

Thank you for loving me in our messy, glorious, human way and for teaching me so much about what love means.

For all these things and far more than I can express in words, I am grateful to you, my friend, and to God who gave us to each other in friendship.

Anam Cara, my Soul Friend, I shall miss your poetry, singing, laughter, courage, honesty, and your deep beauty in this world.

God, help me to keep and to carry all the richness you have given me, to grow it and share it abundantly with the world as you have. And we will have beautiful, hilarious stories to tell and songs to sing together when "we pick up where we left off when we all meet again."

Bobbie was devoted to Amy because Amy truly *saw* her. Amy saw the fierceness and strength under Bobbie's "I'm laughing awkwardly at something so you won't know how much it hurts" exterior. And Bobbie saw the weakness and beauty under Amy's party-girl sarcastic fierceness. In their friendship, Bobbie and Amy were known by each other.

✛

When I was writing *Pastrix,* I told my editor about having an autoimmune disorder from ages twelve to sixteen that caused my eyes to bulge out of my face so much that my eyelids were literally unable to close. I told her about the pain of that particularly unique experience of adolescence. Unhelpfully, I thought, she suggested I write about it.

"Absolutely not," I said.

Once I'd given her a draft of the entire book for its final editing, she read it and then sent it back to me, saying, "Now read this and tell me that isn't an important piece of the story. Why the hell else would you be such a pissed-off kid? Be brave. Tell it." And so, reluctantly, I did.

Of all the inelegant things I wrote about myself in that book— publicly admitting to drug use, alcoholism, deceit, sexual indiscretion, misanthropy, and pretending to be a hero—the pain and alienation of my childhood was the one thing that made me think, *If I tell this, I may die. If I show the encasing under the tattoos, no one will again believe that I am cool.*

Any college freshman in a Psychology 101 class could spot it in under ten minutes, but I didn't realize for a couple of years why so many "losers" were coming to House for All Sinners and Saints, the church with the (supposedly) cool, tattooed lady pastor. Ends up, I *was* attracting people like me. I just didn't want to see it. Some might think the funny, tattooed, sarcastic part of me attracts people to House for All. And that's true for some people, but they're the ones who never seem to stick around.

But the "cool" part of me was never what attracted the people who stayed. The bug-eyed kid with no friends brought them in. The girl who ate all her lunches alone in middle school. The me who had to brace herself every single day against a relentless barrage of insults— the painfully skinny girl who learned to bandage and cover her wounds with anger, cynicism, and colorful language. I had been attracting people like me all along. I was just too arrogant, or too defensive, to admit it.

House for All Sinners and Saints began to make so much more sense to me after that realization. What I really needed at my church, based on the truth inside of me, was to be confronted by whatever it is I was trying to push down, compensate for, and cover up. What I needed was Bobbie.

Though it's boilerplate pop psychology, this fact continues to be disturbingly and consistently true: Whenever people annoy me beyond reason, I can guarantee it's because they're demonstrating something I'd rather not see in myself. Which is to say, I didn't know how to love Bobbie because I didn't know how to stop hiding the parts of myself that she made me face.

There's a parable in Luke's gospel that Jesus tells at a dinner party when he sees how guests were choosing the best places to sit for themselves:

> He said also to the one who had invited him, "When you give a luncheon or a dinner, do not invite your friends or your brothers or your relatives or rich neighbors, in case they may invite you in return, and you would be repaid. But when you give a banquet, invite the poor, the crippled, the lame, and the blind. And you will be blessed, because they cannot repay you, for you will be repaid at the resurrection of the righteous." (14:12–14)

Here Jesus comments on the things we do (or don't do) so that people will think of us in a certain way. And it reminds me of how my friend Caitlin claims that I do actually have really lovely aspects of my

personality—they just aren't my favorite parts. This parable forces
me to examine all the ways I try to project my favorite parts of my
personality—my "coolness," my supposedly badassed, cutting-edge
attitude—hoping people will buy the PR about who I am.

And I'm not alone. This practice of curating parts of one's self is
something many of us do to some degree. We carefully create a persona,
but it's always one that's only partially true. And maintaining this par-
tial truth, this created personality, this assembled "self," can be pretty
exhausting. Facebook is the perfect medium for this bit of artisanship.
It allows us to present an image of ourselves from just the parts of our
lives and personalities we wish to project. This is why we almost never
see updates on Facebook that say: *Spent the evening alone again last
night.* Or: *Wonder if I'll ever be loved.* Or: *Just manipulated my spouse
to get my own way.*

If our Facebook profile picture could be seen as a metaphor for this
pretense, the parable of the dinner party sets Jesus up as the friend who
relentlessly tags unflattering photos of us. Photos where our hair is a
mess, our butt looks big, and one eye is half-closed.

I often think that the effort we put into trying to pretend something about us is true—that we are less than we are or more than we
are or that one aspect of ourselves is the whole story—is based in a fear
of being really known, of being truly seen, as we actually are. Perhaps
we each have a wound, a vulnerable place that we have to protect in
order to survive. And yet sometimes we overcompensate so much for
the things we are trying to hide that no one ever suspects the truth . . .
and then we are left in the true aloneness of never really being known.

In the end, the only real love in the world is found when you let
yourself be truly known. This was the love Amy and Bobbie shared,

loving each other in, through, and beyond what each woman tried to hide or protect.

✦

The film *Almost Famous* tells the story of a young man, William, who finds himself as a reporter on tour with a famous rock band. His conversation with an older writer, Lester, at the end of the film captures this notion perfectly.

William laments that he tried to be cool, that he felt *almost* cool with the guys in the band, even though he ultimately knew he wasn't.

Lester exclaims, "Look, I've met you. You're not cool. But the only true currency in this bankrupt world is what we share with someone else when we're uncool."

At the end of his dinner party parable, Jesus says that when a party is thrown we should invite the lame, the poor, the crippled, and the blind. Might he be suggesting that in God's kingdom we can embrace whatever we are trying to hide or compensate for? In the kingdom of God, we need not cultivate a persona to hide the lame, poor, blind, or crippled parts of us. The unflattering photos. The parts that have nothing to offer, that must rely on others for help.

In other words, the uncool parts of us are exactly what Jesus invites to sit and eat around his table. As though the only true currency in this bankrupt world is what we share with God and each other when we are uncool, lame, blind, poor, and crippled. And as uncomfortable as I am, as you are, to be seen in such a stark and uncompromising light, there is much relief in it. Perhaps it really is safer and even wise in so much of our lives to protect ourselves. But around God's table, and around God's people, you don't have to pretend or overcompensate. You can just be. And in just being, you can, in the fierce and loving eyes of God, be known, be whole, and maybe even find a little rest. Because keeping it all going is just exhausting.

✦

Two weeks after Amy Mack's funeral, Bobbie and I were walking upstairs from "office hours" in the basement of a local coffee shop, a time each week when folks from church gather to just hang out and chat. I'd been on the road speaking at events a great deal, more than is technically healthy for me, and was struggling with the particular exhaustion that comes from having been surrounded by thousands of people who think they know me and yet do not.

When we got outside, Bobbie said, "Hey, I um . . . I have something for you."

She handed me a cloth bag. Inside was a journal, its beautiful tooled-leather cover clearly handmade by Bobbie. It bore the image of Mary Magdalene announcing the Resurrection to the apostles, an image from the Saint Albans Psalter that had been tattooed on my arm during a period in my life when I was responding to my call to be a preacher.

I gasped when I saw it and hugged her for what a passerby might have thought an unusually long time. This was a gift only someone who *saw* me could give; it was so personal and perfect.

"Bobbie. I just . . . um, thank you. Thank you."

"It's for your sabbatical. Please fill it."

I immediately thought of all the times Bobbie had made me uncomfortable, the times I could have visited the hospital more when Amy Mack was sick, the times I had not engaged with Bobbie as I could have. This is why being loved, really loved, can sting a little, reminding us of all the times we have loved poorly or not at all, all the ways in which we have done things that make us feel unworthy of real love.

But I know how to love and appreciate Bobbie now because she and Amy showed me. Bobbie loved Amy because Amy saw her, and once I was able to see Bobbie (and not just see in her the parts of myself I try to pretend aren't there), I loved her too. It's hard not to. She's amazing. And, clearly, Bobbie knows how to love me. This small but amazing act of love—for Bobbie to hand-tool the leather journal for me to use while I was away from my life as a pastor, away from the parish, the readers, the stage—was something only someone who *saw* me could do.

I still show that journal to anyone who will look at it. Like it's a picture of my baby or a report card. I show it off as if to say, "Look. Someone loves me." Someone sees and loves the weird, skinny bug-eyed girl sitting alone at the lunch table. And that girl loves her back.

13

✦

Dirty Feet

large oak tree anchors the center of the Spanish courtyard outside the parish hall in which our liturgies take place at House for All Sinners and Saints. The canopy from its wise branches provides a leafy roof over our heads without it blocking the view of the stars or the warmth of the sun. This tree, as with so many of its fellows, has seen what only trees can: the world as it exists in one place for years passing. Walking past our courtyard tree must surely have once been lovers with eyes only for each other, priests with hurried footsteps, and babies with heads still glistening from their baptisms. This courtyard tree has surely seen old ladies holding mugs of light brown church coffee, homeless folks needing to sit for a minute, and even a few fights over church budgets.

But on Maundy Thursday at House for All Sinners and Saints—the day we remember Jesus's last supper with his disciples, a meal at which he washed the feet of his unreliable friends—the tree sees a lot of feet. And a lot of forgiveness.

Forgiveness of sins is a tricky business. In my childhood I was taught that all the not-perfect things we do or say or think are all tallied up on some big spiritual dry-erase board in heaven. This is, of course, what God mostly busies himself with. A sin is a sin is a sin, I was told. So red marks both for someone who murders and for someone who thinks to herself that her teacher is a real asshole. I was told that when Jesus came and died on the cross he wiped all those red marks away, but before Jesus, we had to get priests to offer sacrifices on our behalf in order for the marks to go away. And let's be honest . . . that's a lot of dead goats and pigeons. So God sent his son to be the sacrifice for everyone once and for all. (I understand why that would be good news for goats and pigeons, but I'm less clear why that's good news for me.) By sacrificing Jesus, God put the eraser in our hands, so that now, if we confess our sins and feel terrible for every bad deed, word, or thought and if we promise not to do, say, or think those things again, then the marks are erased. And when it comes down to it, God is pleased with us only when we have a clean board. Die with marks on it, and you may go to hell. So, you know . . . get busy.

This view of sin and punishment is perhaps not as commonly held now as it was in previous generations, so I'm not sure how many people believe that God is holding a big grudge against them for being bad. Sure, some still believe that in heaven there is a list of good behaviors and bad behaviors and therefore to know that God forgives your sin is to know that God has erased the red marks against you and therefore is no longer mad, which means he won't punish you.

But honestly, I'm much more tortured by my secrets, which eat away at me, than I am concerned about God being mad at me. I'm more haunted by how what I've said and the things I've done have caused harm to myself and others than I am worried that God will punish me for being bad. Because in the end, we aren't punished *for* our sins as much as we are punished *by* our sins.

And sin is just the state of human brokenness in which what we say and do causes these sometimes tiny and sometimes monstrous fractures in our earth, in ourselves, in those we love, and sometimes even in our own bodies. Sin is the self curved in on the self. And it's not something we can avoid entirely.

When I was working as a student hospital chaplain in the mid-aughts, I was called in on a bright Thursday in March to a fetal demise case, which is a polite way of saying a dead baby was still in its mother's womb.

There was no one else in the room when I got there, just the mother, Candy, her grief, and a half-empty pack of Marlboros by her side. I took her hand and said I could sit with her for a while if she'd like, knowing that vapid words of comfort in such a situation fall like slick little stones to the ground and are best just left unspoken.

Without prompting, she explained how this was not her fault and neither was the fact that she didn't have custody of her other four children. That "bitch social worker who doesn't have any kids of her own and doesn't understand nothing" was behind that. And the local cop who had it out for her, and not her own choices, was behind her many arrests.

Methamphetamine does an unmistakable thing to human teeth. And so, through her damaged mouth, came a string of grief-stained words of blame, none of which landed on herself.

After spending half my shift with her, I left that room so very sad. Sad for the loss of the baby. Sad for her childlessness despite a womb that had borne so many. But mostly I was saddened knowing that she won't feel the release of speaking the truth of how we all participate in our own suffering.

✦

When first I started dipping my toes back into Christianity, I hated the confession at the beginning of the liturgy. It felt like the church's way of creating job security: the church makes us feel so bad about ourselves that we then have to go to the church for absolution. But eventually I realized that confession and absolution were pretty similar to my alcohol recovery program, which included an exercise in which you make a searching and fearless moral inventory of yourself and read it aloud to another human being.

In 1992, at the time of my first moral inventory, I was so filled with shame about the things I had done, so filled with self-hatred, that the person I chose to hear me read it aloud was Anna, a woman who was literally dying of AIDS. We'd met at the twelve-step meeting I was attending in New York City during a nine-month period when I had tried and failed to successfully live there. The only reason I trusted her to hear all of my crap was that I was certain she'd not be alive eight or nine weeks later.

We sat in her tiny primary-color-soaked New York apartment while I fidgeted with the papers on which I'd handwritten all my sins. She offered me some tea and after placing a red cup and saucer next to me, she took her seat on a worn easy chair from which she listened to me tell her about all the shit I'd done. Anna's clothes had become so ill-fitting they didn't look like her own and she sat there, kind-faced and patient. Her breath rattled in and out of her lungs as my list of affairs, crimes, and betrayals rattled out of mine.

"Nadia," she said when I'd finally read the last page, "we've all been there and that shit is in the past. Stop carrying it with you into the present." She adjusted her oxygen tube for a minute before continuing. "It's over, girl. And you're gonna be okay."

Having sat across from a frail, emaciated thirty-year-old woman in her tiny studio apartment and spoken aloud all of the things for which I was ashamed, with her taking it all in without judgment and then holding it all for me so that I could let it go, I felt a freedom that nothing else could have given me. Which is why as soon as I was able to stop thinking of forgiveness of sins as the dry-erase situation and start thinking of it as freedom from the bondage of self, everything changed.

✧

On Maundy Thursday we tell the story of how Jesus washed the feet of his friends and commanded us (*Maundy* means "command") to love one another as he has loved us. We wash each other's feet (or hands in the case of Amy Mack, who had once reminded me that her hands *were* her feet) and we celebrate the Eucharist. The foot washing thing is cool, but for me, Maundy Thursday is all about forgiveness of sins.

On the night that Jesus was betrayed by his friends, he first had dinner with them. But before that, he tied the towel of a servant girl around his waist and he washed their feet. And to be clear, this wasn't after they'd tidied up first. Jesus met them where they were: with dirty feet, literally and metaphorically. Hours before his disciples betrayed, denied, and abandoned him, Jesus washed their filthy feet. He knew what was about to go down. In the days and weeks prior, he had tried telling them that he would be betrayed and handed over to suffer and be killed, and they all thought he was crazy. But he knew. As he knelt before his friends and washed their feet, he knew that very night they would do the thing that would torture them for the rest of their lives. They would deny, betray, and hand over their own friend and teacher. They would not be the men and women they wanted to be.

We start out Lent with the acknowledgement of human mortality and a hefty confession of sins at Ash Wednesday, and then for the five

Sundays after, as we stay in the wilderness of Lent, we do not receive absolution again until Maundy Thursday, and when we do, we receive it individually. There is no music playing at this point in the liturgy. In silence, each person walks up—the leaders of the church, my dad, strangers, the cantor, and even my children—they make their way around the large oak tree and the tangled crowd in the courtyard, and I lay my hands on their head and say, "In obedience to the command of our Lord Jesus Christ, I proclaim to you the entire forgiveness of all your sins. Amen."

Sometimes I know what those sins are and sometimes I don't, but every single time, my hands shake. Because this shit is real.

Wanting to get at this idea that God meets us first under the oak tree, when our feet are dirty, not just after we have managed to clean them up, House for All Sinners and Saints has the practice of both foot washing and bleach kit assembly on Maundy Thursday. We sing "Take, O, Take Me As I Am" as we assemble bleach, tourniquets, and condoms into kits for outreach workers, through an underground needle exchange program, to hand to IV drug users on the streets of Denver. This is not a quaint "service project." It is a radical statement that we believe in grace.

✦

Sometimes I think about Candy, and I wonder if she's ever encountered a Denver outreach worker with a bleach kit. Did she ever open a baggie from a clean-handed social worker and see a note under the tourniquet and sterile cooker that said, "You are loved as you are," and did it ever break her heart? Well-meaning notes from church folks aren't miracles and perhaps they all go unnoticed, but even if that's the case, the truth remains: God loves Candy *now*. With dirty feet. Not just after she manages to start making better decisions, not after she washes them herself. God loves us *now*. Me, Anna, Candy, all of us, as we are. Sometimes just the simple experience of knowing this, of knowing that our sin is not what defines us, can finally set us free.

14

***

The Dogs of Good Friday

I couldn't see the dogs, but I could definitely hear them as they violently strained against the chain-link fence, their barking tearing at my nerves. I steadied myself and quietly pulled a few bundles of purple tulips from my blue Honda while my intern, Alex, carefully unloaded House for All Sinners and Saints' large crucifix. We walked up a dark street with no sidewalks or streetlamps toward the house where, a month earlier, twenty-three-year-old Mayra Perez had shot her own children, ages four, two, and one, before turning the gun on herself. Only the two-year-old girl survived. For this young mother, there had not been the hope of dawn, of the light that could come to scatter Good Friday's darkness.

It was 2013 and we were continuing a practice started on our first Good Friday together where, after the liturgy, we gather together at a site where an act of brutal violence had taken place in our city and there we pray and lay down tulips, tulips that had been handed to those entering our Good Friday liturgy a couple of hours earlier and had then been laid at the cross as we sang "Were You There When They Crucified My Lord?" We bring the holy things of the church onto the holy streets of the city because on some level, the violence and despair of Good Friday is still a human reality.

Unfortunately, we've never lacked an opportunity to pay such a visit.

Other parishioners parked on the dark street and joined Alex and me like a slow, quiet flash mob until we all stood near the ground where blood had been spilled and hope had been absent. Eventually there was a circle of forty-five of us, all unnerved by the darkness and the snarling dogs. I was glad for our numbers. Had there been only a handful I'd have been terrified to be in this place. I guess I was terrified anyway.

With both hands, Alex held up the large crucifix, made of tree branches and a realistically painted molded resin body of Jesus, and we began.

✛

Earlier that evening, the cross had been featured in our incense-filled and candlelit Good Friday procession at church, held by the cantor as he chanted, "Behold the life-giving cross on which was hung the Savior of the whole world." The congregation had responded, "Oh come, let us worship him."

We had sat in chairs in tight rows facing each other in a starkly empty space, filled only with incense and an empty altar table draped in black at the center of the room. I sat next to Kate and Megan, and after the cross was laid on the altar in repose, the air didn't move. We didn't move. And then the cantor began to sing Psalm 22, the words of a dying Christ: "My God, my God, why have you forsaken me?" Then, when we sat down, the passion of Jesus Christ from the gospel of John was sung.

The story of Jesus's trial—the thorns twisted into crowns, the flogging, the cries of "crucify him" and "I am thirsty"—is different when it is sung. Some things just have to be sung to be heard fully, so three different voices sang the roles of the narrator, Jesus, and the crowd.

Kate had been to church only three times before coming to House for All Sinners and Saints, but on that night, she sang the Solemn Reproaches at a Good Friday liturgy. Kate is a curvy, brown-haired beauty who loves dragonflies and yoga and often speaks of what the universe is trying to tell her. Her childhood was filled with alcoholism and dysfunction, so Kate is like one of those flowers that manages to grow in garbage.

I met Megan, the other woman who, alongside Kate, sang the leader parts for the Solemn Reproaches, at a local hipster clothing store three years earlier, and I invited her to House for All. Megan, a tattooed rock-'n'-roll maven, was raised Catholic but hadn't gone to church for twenty years. Growing up in New York City gave her a sharp edge, but that edge never really managed to hide her generous heart. Her old red pickup truck sported an array of bumper stickers in the back window, declaring to those driving behind her all the things Megan loves: punk rock band, punk rock band, punk rock band, House for All Sinners and Saints, punk rock band, punk rock band, punk rock band.

These two young women, neither likely to ever be in a church, sat side by side and sang the Solemn Reproaches, a Good Friday rite dating back to the ninth century.

The reproaches all begin with Micah 6:3: "O my people, [O my church,] what have I done to you? How have I offended you? Answer me!" Then each reproach goes on to allude to a biblical grace or gift from God followed by the human response, which is to reject the gift—a human instinct that always ends in the same way: the suffering of God.

O my people, O my church, what have I done to you, or in
what have I offended you? Answer me. I led you forth from the
land of Egypt and delivered you by the waters of baptism, but
you have prepared a cross for your Savior.

The congregation sang the Trisagion (the "thrice holy" of the
Eastern Orthodox tradition) — "Holy God, holy and mighty, holy
and immortal, have mercy upon us" — as a response for each of the
reproaches.

As Kate and Megan sang this ancient chant, it felt as though their
voices were reaching through two thousand years of Christian faith
and bringing back into the room with them the full force of humanity's
folly; we humans don't really know how to respond to the kind of
grace and love shown us in Jesus Christ. Each reproach built in force
upon the last, as did the congregation's sung response. And somehow
the truth of God and humanity, the truth of a gift and the rejection
of a gift, was made real in the vibrations of our singing. So that even
the most cynical and nonreligious among us for those moments could
not keep from weeping for the ways in which we sometimes reject
goodness, turn from love, and make choices that no one who loves us
would ever make on our behalf. But it wasn't guilt we were feeling. At
least not the church-made kind. I know what that feels like, and this
was different.

Because Good Friday is not about us trying to "get right with God."
It is about us entering the difference between God and humanity and
just touching it for a moment. Touching the shimmering sadness of
humanity's insistence that we can be our own gods, that we can be pure
and all-powerful. Some may think that spirituality means attaining a
disembodied transcendent state somewhere up in the ether. But that's

not where we find God . . . that's just where we try to be like God and that's different. Good Friday is a stark and unapologetic display of remorse. Remorse for the way in which humanity kills ourselves and the creation and love and God him/herself.

The Good Friday experience is one of feeling the pain of an entirely unfiltered reality. It is as if the atmosphere, the protective layer between us and the sun, has for a moment disappeared and we are being burned. I wonder if God is like the sun in that way and is the reason Moses could not look at God, because we need a protective barrier. We need God for light and warmth, but we also need some protection from God—not because God is an angry bastard, as some would have us believe, but because we would cripple under God's truth, unfiltered. Which is why we do the Good Friday liturgy only once a year. None of us could bear it more often than that.

Yet to never touch the truth of these things is to live only halfway.

After we sat in our rows facing the altar and sang of the death of Jesus, we began the adoration of the cross—a time that closes the Good Friday liturgy when worshipers are invited to show their respect, to solemnly approach the altar, first just one person, then several, and finally ten or so at a time. Many simply laid at the cross the purple tulips they received for this purpose, others touched it lovingly or kissed it, and some even unselfconsciously bowed on the ground in prayer, pulled down into the dirt like only the devastated can do.

Then we drove to the junkyard-dog-menaced site of a double murder/suicide, and for the second time that evening our crucifix was placed into the center of those gathered, because Good Friday is not just a single event in history that we choose to remember a couple of days before Easter. On some level, although we can't handle the pain of acknowledging it, Good Friday happens every day.

After singing in the parish hall with heart and tears and shaking voices, "Were you there when they crucified my Lord?" we stood at this horrible site and asked our crucified Lord, "Were you there when Mayra Perez took three lives?"

As people who believe in a God who suffered violence and affliction and responded in love, we had to believe, yes.

Then, with purple tulips in our hands and Alex still holding the cross, we sang the first note of the Trisagion, *"Holy God, holy and mighty, holy and immortal, have mercy upon us."* Each of us then took an unsure hand of tulips and laid them lovingly on the ground as again we sang, *"Holy God, holy and mighty, holy and immortal, have mercy upon us."*

And suddenly, as if it were staged, the dogs stopped barking. As if their barks had also been pleadings for God's mercy, and they were grateful for us to take over for a few minutes. Then, the moment we stopped praying, they took up their banner of protest and petition and resumed their cacophony.

Without speaking, we left the barking dogs, walked away with the cross, and left the tulips there on that cold and holy ground. Then we headed home to await the dawn.

In the car on the way back, after a few minutes of silence, I asked Alex, "What the hell just happened?"

"I have no idea. But I know it did."

✤

A week later I got a call from Laurel, who works for a faith-based community-organizing group.

"One of our gun-violence prevention clergy called me this morning," Laurel said. "One of the families in the neighborhood told him that a group of random Christians came to the area of the murder/suicide singing, praying, and bearing a cross. He wanted to make sure that we knew the neighborhood noticed. Pastor Tyler wanted you to know how grateful he is for what House for All did and how you all helped to bring a sense of healing."

It was so dark. We had no idea anyone was watching.

15

Vignettes from an Easter Vigil

I. THE MELTED REMAINS

Twenty-two hours after throwing tulips on the cold ground, we gathered on Holy Saturday, in darkness, and again outside in the courtyard, where we were washed and forgiven on Maundy Thursday. But this time, we gathered around a fire pit, the light of which represents the hope of resurrection.

A new paschal candle is lit by this fire and the light is then shared with all who stand, hovering against the wind, candles in hand. Throughout the coming year this candle will be lit whenever there are white paraments [9] displayed at church: at baptisms and funerals as well as on Easter and All Saints. But tonight it is new. And yet for our community it is also always old, formed from the melted remains of a year's worth of candles, flecked with glorious imperfections.

II. THE BEES, GOD'S SERVANTS

Religiously speaking, Andie had mostly been either nothing or Unitarian when she joined seven other people in starting House for All with me in the fall of 2007. She's a big, tattooed, beautiful queer girl with a stunning contralto voice.

---

9. Paraments are the cloth coverings on the altar, the pulpit, and the pastor's stole (a scarf-like garment).

About six months after joining, she texted me, "Hey Rev, I may need some pastoral care."

We met the next day for coffee, and when I asked her what was up she said, "I think I'm having a crisis of faith."

To which I thought, *What the hell does that look like for a Unitarian?*

"Yeah," she continued. "I think I believe in Jesus." Oh. That's what it looks like.

"I'm so sorry," I replied. "But sometimes Jesus just hunts your ass down and there's nothing you can do about it."

Now, five years later, during the Easter Vigil, as we enter our dim worship space from the courtyard holding small candles lit by the new paschal candle, it is Andie's voice that fills the room chanting the Exsultet, an ancient chant about the Easter Vigil. Occasionally she sings the refrain, "This is the night . . . ," and the congregation responds, "This is the night." The haunting chant tells of the light of the paschal candle as it reflects the Light of Christ, including (my favorite part) thanking God for the bees, God's servants:

> We sing the glories of this pillar of fire,
> the brightness of which is not diminished
> even when its light is divided and borrowed.
>
> For it is fed by the melting wax which the bees, your
>   servants,
> have made for the substance of this candle.
> This is the night [This is the night]
> in which heaven and earth are joined—things human
>   and things divine.

If you find yourself singing praises for the bees, God's servants, whose work went into making a paschal candle, then Jesus very well may have hunted your ass down. And there is nothing to be done but to keep singing on Holy Saturday as the notes join in to things human and things divine.

III. Dry Bones

On Sundays at House for All we chant a psalm and read from the gospel, an epistle, and a Hebrew Bible text, but at the Great Vigil of Easter, traditionally there are twelve readings. One night a year we tell each other the great stories of our faith so that we can remember who we are. Once a year we gather around the fire of a beautifully imperfect candle and tell each other about God and God's people.

Stephen, our aging-movie-star-looking Fortune 500 company guy, wanted to do the Valley of the Dry Bones reading from the book of Ezekiel.

When Stephen walked up with a single sheet of paper, the light bouncing off his perfect head of salt-and-pepper hair, he said to us that he felt emotionally dead and that for this condition, nothing makes a difference:

No website;
No relationship;
No Mac computer or iPhone;
No exercise, no diet, no supplement;
No job, office, or title on my business card;
No amount of Diet Coke, good scotch, or bad beer;
No self-help book, therapist, or self-improvement class;

No car, house, or any other status symbol I can think
    to buy;
No movie or video game, and no matter how truly
    awesome Doctor Who is.

They have all done nothing more than temporarily anesthetize
the longing in my soul to be complete, to be whole, to be
connected, to be okay, to love and be loved as I am now with too
much weight, too much debt, too much depression, too much
gray, too much geek, and not enough of everything else.

And I despair that my trip on this rock flying around the sun at
sixty-seven thousand miles an hour is just some sort of sick
cosmic joke.

But then I remember. I remember the Valley. The
    Valley of the Dry Bones.

God is talking to the prophet Ezekiel and guides him into
something resembling a massive open grave.

It's a valley covered, from one end to the next, with nothing but
humanity at its core—dry bones. In this valley there is abso-
lutely no hope of life.

God tells Ezekiel to cry out, cry out to those dry bones, cry out to
God's children. Tell them to rise, tell them to rise, tell them to
listen to God and rise. They listen.

*And God lifts them up, puts them back together, and breathes
into them. And they breathe anew. And God fills them with the
Spirit. And where there was once death, hopelessness, and
despair, there is new life.*

*In hearing that, there is light. There is hope. And that is
sufficient.*

That night it *was* sufficient. It was sufficient for Stephen, the ri-
diculously successful man with debilitating depression, to lay bare the
truth of the dryness of his bones to a room of friends and strangers so
that they and he might hear the story of how sometimes the very breath
of God can put back together, bone by bone, that which we think is
dead.

A week later, Stephen admitted to me that his reading was probably
not something most corporate vice presidents do, but that he felt somehow safe in our community and wanted to be open to something bigger
than himself.

Sometimes I wonder if that is what faith is: risking an openness to
something bigger than ourselves—something from which we are made
and yet without which we are not complete, our origin and our
completion.

IV. The Fiery Furnace Wears Orange Chuck Taylors

I was completely unprepared for what happened in the final storytell-
ing: the deliverance from the fiery furnace in the book of Daniel.

A group of five folks, all over the age of forty, performed a hilarious rendition of the story. The main characters, Shadrach, Meshach, and Abednego, all in choir robes, sunglasses, and shiny bling in the form of S, M, and A adorning their chests, formed a doo-wop group and sang their story. Hilarious. But nothing compared to the part of the story when the king throws them into a fiery furnace.

Mist from a smoke machine covered the stage and out popped Amy Clifford. Amy, the behind-the-scenes detail person, in all her strong, tattooed, zaftig, southern lady glory, *was* the fiery furnace. She wore a bright orange minidress adorned with large round sequins that moved with the light, a huge black wig, orange Chuck Taylors, and paper flames attached to her hands. I'm not sure how long it took before people stopped belly laughing, but it was a long-ass time. And having that moment of hilarity was as important as anything else we did that Holy Week.

V. Moldy Alleluias

The word *alleluia* is neither said nor sung during the season of Lent. In fact, in some churches, any cloth banners that bear the word *alleluia* are buried on Transfiguration Sunday (the week before Lent starts) and are not dug up again until the Easter Vigil as a symbol of death and resurrection.

The first time we dug up an Alleluia banner after the Easter Vigil's Litany of Saints, it was difficult to decide if the banner was more tacky than moldy or more moldy than tacky. Some said tacky, since on that first Transfiguration Sunday when we realized we did not actually *own* an Alleluia banner to bury, we proceeded to just set out whatever craft supplies were on hand—glitter, glue guns, markers, and tiny little pompoms—and let everyone have a go at making one on the spot (including my then nine-year-old son, Judah, who drew the one thing he knew how to: Garfield the cat's face upside down above the *u* in *Alleluia*). The result was hideous. Free-form Alleluia banners aren't cool; they just end up looking a bit like sparkly craft projects made by mentally ill toddlers.

We were trying so hard to be groovy that first year, eschewing the more common practice of "burying" the Alleluia *inside* the church. That would not do.

What I can tell you is that if you wrap a tacky Garfield-faced homemade glue-gunned Alleluia banner in linen and bury it in the ground for forty days, when the congregation at the Easter Vigil returns from the Litany of Saints and the children frantically dig at the ground, pulling the fabric bundle from the dirt, that banner will be moldy as hell. Black fuzzy dots will freckle the upside-down Garfield face and accompany the tiny pompoms. But that's okay. In a way, all our alleluias are a little tacky and/or a little moldy.

VI. Light

Jim never participates in the Litany of Saints. He just thinks it's too weird. He was robbed by the Thief in an Advent night—robbed of his certainty that church was not for him—but Jesus did not manage to steal his Baptist-boy suspicion of things being a bit too "Catholic."

The rest of us gathered back outside with a thurible of incense and slowly processed around the outside of the church, chanting the names in our book of the dead, inviting the great cloud of witnesses to now witness with us the resurrection of our Lord.

I chanted, "Saint Peter and Mary Magdalene."

And the congregation responded, "Come celebrate with us."

"Vincent van Gogh and Martin Luther King Jr."

"Come celebrate with us."

"Amy Mack and Billy."

"Come celebrate with us."

Jim stayed behind to lead the "flower fairies," those who stay back to prepare the space for when everyone returns. When their work was done, and when the kids, having returned from the Litany of Saints, had unburied the Alleluia, Jim heard the three knocks at the closed door of the church and swung it open, quickly moving out of the way as people streamed through, singing "Alleluia" together for the first time since Lent started.

We entered a room now filled with light and Easter lilies and sang like only people who have been forgiven and washed each other's feet and touched betrayal and entered death and thrown tulips in the darkness and held the smallest candles and been reminded of the story of God and God's people and invited all the faithful who have gone before them to join in witnessing the resurrection could sing.

We celebrated the Eucharist and had as many baptisms as possible. When the Vigil had ended, we threw a dance party. We danced with relief and joy and transcendence. And resurrection.

Therefore, in this night of grace, receive, O God,
our praise and thanksgiving for the light of the
resurrection of our Lord Jesus Christ, reflected
in the burning of this candle.

We sing the glories of this pillar of fire, the brightness
of which is not diminished even when its light is
divided and borrowed.

For it is fed by the melting wax which the bees, your
servants, have made for the substance of this candle.

This is the night in which heaven and earth are
joined—things human and things divine.

We, therefore, pray to you, O God, that this candle,
burning to the honor of your name, will continue
to vanquish the darkness of night and be mingled
with the lights of heaven.

May Christ the Morning Star find it burning, that
Morning Star who never sets, that Morning Star
who, rising from the grave, faithfully sheds light
on the whole human race.

16

·:·

Charcoal Fires and Jail Cells

I never should have checked my e-mail while I was on vacation. Especially a vacation in Fake Mexico. (What we call "Fake Mexico" is geographically located in the country of Mexico but is in fact just a really nice resort named Grand Mayan Riviera Maya.)

It was the second time my husband, Matthew, and I had gone to Fake Mexico with our friends Jay and Annie, who, like us, are also what you call Lutheran pastors. So the week after Easter 2013, the four of us checked into a resort with a single plan: Read beach books while lying in palapas by the pool. Eat good food. Hang out. Repeat.

I'm constitutionally incapable of sleeping in, even on vacation in Fake Mexico, so on day three I stopped trying and just made my early morning coffee, paid the 120 pesos for a day of wireless access, sat down on the lime green sofa, and opened Facebook. I had a message from a young pastor who had been on the Holy Land tour group with me that just said, "I want to make sure you've heard about what happened to Bruce."

Perhaps one of the least helpful messages in all of message history. What the hell happened to Bruce, the bishop I had pastored while his wife was dying, the man who had led our trip to the Holy Land only five months ago? Was he dead? Injured?

I went to Bruce's Facebook page and all I saw was one post from a friend saying, "We heard about the accident and we are praying for you." Shit. Bruce was hurt and I was in Mexico. My phone couldn't get a signal. Finally I found Nick online. Nick used to work in the same church as Bruce and the two were close friends.

In a brief exchange on instant message, I learned that, two nights earlier, Bruce got behind the wheel of his car with what tests would later show to be a higher than legal blood-alcohol level, lost control, and hit and killed a fifty-two-year-old mother of three. And by the time I found out, from my luxurious room in a resort in Mexico, Bruce was sitting alone in jail; it was an image I could not get out of my mind. He was in jail. And he'd killed someone.

I usually know better than to preach the day after I return from vacation, knowing that I will inevitably be thinking about the sermon for days before I am supposed to, but in this case I forgot. I started working on my sermon on the plane ride home.

"Can I get you something to drink?" the woman in her sixties in a United Airlines uniform asked as she handed me a napkin. For a split second I thought about asking for a vodka and soda, an insane thought for a recovering alcoholic. Every time one of my friends dies from alcoholism or has some kind of booze-related tragedy, I both recoil from and am perversely attracted to the stuff.

"Coffee. And a little milk. Thanks."

The gospel text for that Sunday was the Resurrection story from John where the disciples are fishing in a boat and they see Jesus grilling fish on the beach and Peter (Jesus's denier) swims to him. Jesus asks Peter if he loves him and Peter, three times, says yes.

But my attempts at focusing on the text were interrupted over and over again by the image of my loving friend Bruce sitting in a jail cell. I could not keep from thinking how completely filled with remorse, shame, and fear he must have been. And at the same time I could not keep from thinking about the innocent life he had taken, and my gut churned at the whole sick, saddening mess of it all.

In times when we have no words, when we don't know what to think because we are feeling too many things all at once, there is always the liturgy, the words of God's people that have rung through the millennia and that can speak on our behalf—words we can borrow for ourselves.

I just kept saying, *Kyrie eleison, Christe eleison, Kyrie eleison.* (Lord have mercy, Christ have mercy, Lord have mercy.) On that flight home to Denver from Fake Mexico, I fidgeted by lifting the metal tab of my seatbelt up and down—releasing and then catching, releasing and then catching—and silently chanted over and over, *Kyrie eleison.* No other words, no other thoughts, would suffice.

We sing it every week, the Kyrie, the one piece of the Christian Mass that is still in Greek. For some reason it never made it over to Latin like the rest of the liturgy did.

But what do we *mean* when we say, "Lord have mercy"?

Some may say we're asking God to not punish us for our sin, to not rain down fury and violent retribution on us. And maybe there's a place for that. Maybe asking for God's mercy is like saying, we beg you for your mercy to be with us, because ours is not enough. We ask for your wisdom to be with us, your loving-kindness to be with us, because we just don't have enough of our own. And we keep messing everything up. It seems that we are especially moved to beg this of God in situations where we are overwhelmingly aware of our shortcomings and smallness.

Peter surely understood this need for mercy if anyone did. He had been a common fisherman when Jesus walked by and said, "Follow me." Peter dropped his nets and everything he had known and followed this Jesus of Nazareth. And with him, walking the road together, Peter had seen great things. Miraculous wonders, healings, acts of power and grace. Peter was the first to call Jesus the Messiah. He was, above all, earnest in his devotion.

And yet, when it came down to it, Peter, like so many of us, was unable to live up to his own values and ideals. When the hour of Jesus's betrayal and death came, Peter did not bravely stay by Jesus's side. He chose instead to anonymously warm himself by a nearby charcoal fire. But you just can't warm feet that have gone that cold. And he did not go unnoticed, as he had hoped, because three times he was asked by passersby, "Wait, you know him, don't you?" and three times Peter said, "I do not." He loved Jesus, yet in Jesus's hour of need, Peter denied he even knew him. He was tested and he was found wanting. *Kyrie eleison.* Lord have mercy.

When really shitty things happen and we still must go on with our lives, it's hard to focus. Even when I was trying to put the image of a middle-aged woman dead alongside the road and Bruce inside a jail cell out of my mind so I could focus on my sermon, the images kept creeping back like they were hacking a signal into my brain.

But sometimes the thing that keeps buzzing around my head, that I keep swatting to go away so I can write a sermon, actually ends up *being* the sermon. Bruce wasn't a distraction from me thinking about Peter. Bruce *was* Peter.

Could Peter have been filled with anything but unfiltered remorse and regret and self-loathing? How could Peter have lived with himself after what he had done? How many times after Jesus died did Peter replay those hours in his head, wishing beyond hope that he could just go back and change them? Rewrite his own past? Be the man he wished he had been? Lord, have mercy. Who among us can't relate to *that* feeling?

What could possibly have filled every inch of Bruce's jail cell except remorse, regret, self-loathing, and wishing he could just go back in time and not get in that car? If only he could rewrite the past. If only he could not have done that horribly negligent thing that day, a mother of three would be alive, her family would have her at home to love and cherish for years to come, and Bruce would not be facing years in prison and the emotional lead vest of knowing he had taken a life. He could still be doing his ministry of pastoring, helping Palestinian Christians, mourning his late wife, Cynthia, in the bed they had shared, supporting a hospital in India, and just generally being really good at loving people. But that was not going to happen. There is enough tragedy in this story to go around and for everyone to have seconds.

All I know is that while Bruce cannot rewrite his actions from the week of April 7, 2013, and a beloved wife and mother will always be gone to her husband and children, we simply have to cling tightly to the truth that God can redeem it. That is not to minimize the unspeakable loss of a life. That is not to minimize the need for justice. But God is a God of Easter. When Peter jumps into the sea and encounters Jesus on the beach grilling fish over a charcoal fire, I imagine Peter has an olfactory-triggered memory of another charcoal fire. A charcoal fire around which he warmed himself with his own self-protection and fear. Denying his Lord and warming his hands. His own smell of shame.

But the resurrected Christ does such an unbearably loving and merciful thing. He does not rebuke Peter for failing him in his time of need. Instead he gives Peter breakfast, and then he gives Peter three chances to proclaim his love, one for each of his denials.

"Do you love me, Peter?"

With the smell of charcoal in his nostrils, could Peter possibly have answered "yes" without tears in his eyes?

"I have failed you, Lord, and denied you in your hour of death despite everything in me that knew it was wrong, but yes. Three times yes. I love you, Lord. Have mercy upon me."

As I sat on the airplane, fiddling with my seatbelt and thinking of Peter on that beach, I began to see Jesus with Bruce. Bruce, filled with shame and remorse, and Jesus handing him a Clif bar and asking him three times, "Do you love me?"

✦

The adjective so often coupled with mercy is the word *tender,* but God's mercy is not tender; this mercy is a blunt instrument. Mercy doesn't wrap a warm, limp blanket around offenders. God's mercy is the kind that kills the thing that wronged it and resurrects something new in its place. In our guilt and remorse, we may wish for nothing but the ability to rewrite our own past, but what's done cannot, will not, be undone.

But I am here to say that in the mercy of God it can be redeemed. I cling to the truth of God's ability to redeem us more than perhaps any other. I have to. I need to. I want to. For when we say "Lord have mercy," what else could we possibly mean than this truth?

✦

And to say "Lord have mercy, Christ have mercy, Lord have mercy" is to lay our hope in the redeeming work of the God of Easter as though our lives depended on it. Because they do. It means that we are an Easter people, a people who know that resurrection, especially in and among the least likely people and places, is the way that God redeems even the biggest messes we make—mine, Peter's, Bruce's.

17

Judas Will Now Take Your Confession

I once sat at the deathbed of a friend to hear her confession and bring her the Eucharist. She was in her seventies, dying of emphysema and needing a clergyperson. That the clergyperson was me was both ironic and poetic, since twenty years earlier, this same woman, Suzanne Lynch, had basically saved my ass. I was a fucked up kid trying to get sober, and she was a lawyer who lived in the nice part of town and who saw in me something no one else (especially myself) could see. She dared to think I could be something more than the angry, alcohol-dependent mess I was in that moment. I had nowhere else to go and could barely pay for my own groceries when Suzanne invited me to live in her spare bedroom while I tried to get my shit together.

And then two decades later, I sat by her modern recliner in the living room of a seniors' high-rise in Denver, ready for her to confess her sins to me. On the coffee table next to us, issues of the *New York Times* were stacked in faltering layers beside medical supplies and family photos.

"Suzanne, tell me the things that weigh on your conscience," I said to her after having indulged in an appropriate amount of small talk.

"Well, let's define conscience first."

"Bullshit, President Clinton," I replied. "You're avoiding the question."

She gave a raised eyebrow but didn't have the lawyer's fight in her anymore, so she resigned to the inevitable and said, with a brevity I'd not experienced in Suzanne before, the things she had done that troubled her. Some were funny, others sad, and one was particularly painful. But I did not look away from this frustrating, brilliant, strange woman. I heard her secrets while holding her bruised, papery hand. I asked her if she believed that the word of forgiveness that I was about to proclaim to her was from God.

"I believe."

And then I proclaimed to her the word of God: that she is forgiven. She is not the sum total of her mistakes. God is more powerful than her fuck-ups.[10]

Suzanne's shaking hand wiped away her tears. "I feel unbelievably lighter," she said. Suzanne felt what Judas Iscariot never had the chance to feel.

After Peter denied Jesus, he experienced Easter, but after Judas betrayed Jesus, he bought a field, tripped and fell, and his guts burst open. He died alone in a field of blood. He died knowing that he was a sinner and perhaps thinking that God did not want him.

There was no Easter for Judas. There was no Resurrection. There

---

10. It should be noted that proclaiming God's forgiveness to someone as a "word from God" is categorically different from saying to someone, "God put it on my heart to tell you that you need to [fill in the blank]." At several points in the Gospels, Jesus says to proclaim forgiveness of sins in his name. "You are forgiven" is what we can use his authority to say to one another. Too often people try to use God's name to lend authority to their opinions and personal hang-ups and ambitions. This is vanity, as in using the Lord's name in vain.

was no light shining which the darkness could not overcome. Judas never got to be filled with joy and disbelief at Pentecost like those in the upper room. He never got to stick his fingers in the wounds of God. He never got to eat sacramental broiled fish on a beach, served to him by the resurrected Christ. Judas never experienced the defeat of sin and death revealed in the breaking of the bread. He chose death before seeing that death was done for. Our brother Judas.

But was what he did so unforgivable? How is it that Judas, who betrayed Jesus once and was filled with remorse, became the villain, while Peter, who denied Jesus three times and wept bitterly, became the rock on which the church was built? When it comes down to it, what is the difference between Peter and Judas? Well, maybe nothing. And maybe there's not a whole lot of difference between us and them too.

But we get to share something with Peter that Judas never got to experience and it's the thing that could have made all the difference. In Judas's isolation, he never availed himself to the means of grace. Judas carried with him into that field the burden of not experiencing God's grace because he was removed from the community in which he could hear it. In Judas's ears there never was placed a word of grace. And let me tell you, that's not something the sinner can create for him or herself. It is next to impossible in isolation to manufacture the beautiful, radical grace that flows from the heart of God to God's broken and blessed humanity. As human beings, there are many things we can create for ourselves: entertainment, stories, pain, toothpaste, maybe even positive self-talk. But it is difficult to create this thing that frees us from the bondage of self. We cannot create for ourselves God's word of grace. We must tell it to each other. It's a terribly inconvenient and oftentimes uncomfortable way for things to happen. Were we able to receive the word of God through pious, private devotion—through quiet personal

time with God—the Christian life would be far less messy. But, as Paul
tells us, faith comes through hearing, and hearing implies having someone right there doing the telling.

Sometimes this comes in the form of someone reminding us of
God's weirdly gracious nature—like when my friend Caitlin said,
"Nadia, Jesus died for our sins. Including that one"—and sometimes it
comes in the form of a spoken confession and absolution. But sometimes, I believe that God's word of grace can also come through simple,
imperfect everyday human love.

✦

The year I started House for All, when I was still a seminarian, I had
a contentious meeting with a denominational bureaucrat who was
displeased that I used swear words (gasp!) on my personal blog. I was
summoned into his office, where he made thinly veiled threats to my
candidacy for ordination and advised me to change my ways. I, of
course, refused.

I walked out of that corporate office building nestled among the
PR firms and media outlets in Denver's downtown power grid and sat
in my Honda CR-V. I had to wring my hands around my steering
wheel like it was the neck of an enemy for a good long while before I
was able to start the car and make the four-mile drive home. A half hour
later, I stood in the kitchen of my urban 1940s brick ranch and cried,
ranting to my friend Jay on the phone.

I began the conversation manically pacing between the fridge and
the dinner table, but by the end of it I was sitting on the floor in the
corner of the kitchen with my knees pulled into my chest. Jay and I had
known each other for really only nine months (this was years before we

vacationed together with our spouses in Fake Mexico), but he and his wife, Annie, had quickly become close friends.

"Jay, I'm dying here. How dare he? Is he really going to stop me from doing this church thing just because he doesn't think pastors should use the word *bullshit*? Give me a fucking break." I was in full-on rage mode, which I now know is usually just a cover for when I'm full-on scared.

He talked me down, but not all the way. Before he hung up—and I know this was nothing extraordinary—he said, "I love you, Nadia." It broke something in me. We'd not had that kind of friendship before that, the kind where you casually say you love the other person before hanging up. But we did now. And there was something about *hearing it* that was so different than just imagining it to be true. To hear I was loved meant something very particular because of the context in which I heard it, as though Jay was saying, "You are a mess, and you are loved. You have a little issue with anger, and you are loved. I've not even known you that long, and you are loved. You think you are going through this alone but you are wrong, and you are loved. The thing you are experiencing right now seems so big, but what is bigger is that you are loved."

This, like hearing you are forgiven, is something we need each other for.

One of my parishioners, Jeff, recently posted this on our church's Facebook group page:

I struggle with despising people . . . and not even for very good reasons. That guy in the massive pickup who's tailgating me, the smarmy Boulder business types eating hundred-dollar lunches, the horrifically overconfident mom sharing her conversation with the entire coffee shop. I somehow find the energy to mentally eviscerate such people every single day. I'm a hater.

I realize that I do this. And I realize that I do this because I'm a person who, well, does this sort of thing. And how do you become something that you're not?

I've been looking for tools to help me break out of this ridiculous cycle, something to help me see others as more than caricatures or embodiments of trends I despise. And I found such a tool, when I served some of you communion on a recent Sunday at House for All. I looked at you, gave you bread, and said, "Child of God, the body of Christ, broken for you."

Child of God.

Child of God.

We're all children of God. And we've been given the authority, even the duty, to declare that to each other.

And so I find myself on US 36, where another asshole is embodying so much that I despise, and in my mind, I bless them. I look in their eyes, hold up the bread, and say, "Child of God . . ."

Jeff, like so many of us, is changed by the word of grace that he hears in church. He is formed by the Word of God.[11] He is given a place where he is told by others that he is a child of God. He is given a place where he can look other people in the eye, other annoying, inconsistent, arrogant people in the eye, hand them bread, and say, "Child of God,

---

11. One Lutheran teaching that is enormously helpful and wonderful is our understanding of what is meant by the phrase "the Word of God." To us, the Word of God is, first and foremost, Jesus, the Word made flesh. Secondly, the Word of God is any way in which the story of God's self-revelation in Jesus is told to people (thus the importance of hearing). Thirdly, the Word of God is the way in which the Bible tells us who the Triune God is.

the body of Christ, given for you," and then he, in his own arrogant inconsistencies, has a frame of grace through which to see even the people he can't stand. I argue that this wouldn't just happen alone.

This is why we have Christian community. So that we can stand together under the cross and point to the gospel. A gospel that Bonhoeffer said is "frankly hard for the pious to understand. Because this grace confronts us with the truth saying: You are a sinner, a great, desperate sinner, now come as the sinner you are to a God who loves you."

God wants you, you in your imperfect, broken, shimmering glory.

Maybe, after he had fucked up royally, nobody said to Judas, "You are a sinner, a great, desperate sinner, now come as the sinner you are to a God who loves you" even though, as Jeff reminded me, we have the authority and duty to say such things to one another.

How might that early Christian community have been different if Judas had received forgiveness, as the rest of them did? Again and again Jesus had said they should preach forgiveness of sins in his name.

Maybe Judas was destined to betray Jesus. Maybe it couldn't have gone down in any other way than it did. But maybe Judas chose death too soon. Maybe he didn't avail himself of the means of God's grace, and maybe his community never sought him out and offered it. Maybe extending the Word of God's forgiveness to Judas was simply too painful for the disciples because, like with the townspeople who became angry when the Gerasene demoniac was clothed and in his right mind, it was easier to identify Judas as the problem. *Judas* is the traitor . . . not us. Maybe Judas's community failed him.

And if they failed him, I hope they confessed their sin. And I hope they heard the ringing freedom of the very forgiveness and grace they were charged with proclaiming to the world. Because they needed it. And you need it and, trust me, I need it.

We have to hear again and again who God is for us and what God has done on our behalf. We must free each other from bondage through our confession and forgiveness.

I think this is why we at House for All Sinners and Saints sometimes say that we are religious but not spiritual. *Spiritual* feels individual and escapist. But to be *religious* (despite all the negative associations with that word) is to be human in the midst of other humans who are as equally messed up and obnoxious and forgiven as ourselves. It allows us, when confronted both with assholes in SUVs or by our own intolerances, to hold up bread in our mind's eye and say, "Child of God." And sometimes it can look a whole lot like using imperfect love to help keep each other's guts from exploding. So I come to church with my churning gut and I hear that I am forgiven and I again hear of a God who climbs down from heaven to enter the pain and beauty of humanity. I come and hear of a God who climbs up from the earth still stinking of the grave and offers his body for us so that we might in turn be his body in the world because there are fields of blood all around us. There are the abandoned spaces of loss and loathing and remorse in which God's beloved are isolated.

We must be little preachers for one another, and, as my parishioner Jeff expressed, we actually have the *authority* to remind each other of the gospel and defy the darkness of living in a broken world by pointing to the light of Christ. We all need to have our bruised, papery hands held while someone else says, "You are forgiven, and you are loved."

✢

Ever since considering the question, what's the difference between Judas and Peter,[12] I've wondered what would've happened if Judas would have had a forgiving encounter with the resurrected Christ in the same way Peter did. What would've happened if Judas had heard in his ears a word of grace just for him, a word he could not create for himself. Would he still have died at his own hand?

Proclaiming the purifying, forgiving love of God is what I call preaching the gospel. But in a way, it's really only preaching if the one doing the proclaiming hears it too. As I sat by Suzanne, knowing who I had been twenty years ago, I knew I needed to hear the word of forgiveness myself, given what a jerk I had been back in the day.

Holding Suzanne's hand, I couldn't help but think back to two decades earlier when Suzanne's guest bedroom was the only place I had to lay my head. I recalled that back then, during breakfast, I'd wear sleeveless Public Enemy shirts and make as little eye contact as possible, while still passably looking like I was listening to one of her stories or rants. This woman was giving me a free place to live, and yet I somehow resented having to make real conversation with her. I wasn't exactly the most gracious guest. But, twenty years later, I wore a black clergy shirt, and I gave the woman in the recliner my full attention. And I let myself feel comforted by the knowledge that no matter how much of a miserable ingrate I had been to her, God could somehow redeem me and her and our stories and our sin. And I could sit at her side and proclaim this to her a few days before her death as she took some of her final struggling breaths.

Several years before I heard Suzanne's confession, I took her out to

---

12. Which I originally heard from the brilliant Dr. Stephen Paulson at Luther Seminary.

lunch. I thanked her for taking me in and told her that I wished I could repay her somehow. To which she said, "Well, just live your life, kiddo. That's plenty."

And this is it. This is the life we get here on earth. We get to give away what we receive. We get to believe in each other. We get to forgive and be forgiven. We get to love imperfectly. And we never know what effect it will have for years to come. And all of it . . . all of it is completely worth it.

18

⋯⋯ ❖ ⋯⋯

The Best Shitty Feeling
in the World

Australia seems like a really faraway Canada, just with funnier animals." I was saying this to Jane, my spiritual director, as I tried to explain the conundrum I had caused regarding a speaking tour I had agreed to do. "If I wanted to be around poorly dressed white people speaking English, I could just stay home."

Jane is a self-possessed woman in her seventies who has written several books on prayer, and yet she has never, in all the years I've been seeing her, suggested I pray more. For this, I love her. She mostly just listens and occasionally "invites" me to consider something I would never allow myself to consider on my own, like the idea that I am a good person and people *aren't* out to get me. She never fails to offer me a glass of water and a seat in her little sunlit office, tucked away in the back of her 1920s bungalow, where I've cried, realized big things, bored myself, and said the same words more than a dozen times. Through all of this, Jane faithfully listens and tries to show me that I am not a horrible person. I'd refuse to believe this from almost anyone else, because almost anyone else is unfamiliar with the blacker parts of my heart. But

Jane has known me for so long that I trust her, even when she speaks words I secretly find suspicious.

I was explaining to her that Australia wasn't a place I'd always been dying to see. But the real problem was that, without knowing it, I had booked my Down Under speaking tour for the weekend when two of my parishioners were having their wedding—a wedding I had already agreed to officiate. Oops.

My conflict was the product of something so many of us face. Like basically every other adult I know who is trying to balance more than one role—being both a new mom and an employee; being a boss and also the one who is caring for a demented, elderly parent; being someone trying to get sober and someone who also has to keep practicing law at the same time—I never feel like I'm getting everything done or am ever pleasing everyone in my life. It's such a common feeling that it's almost boring to talk about it. But when it's you in the middle, it feels excruciating.

The demands on my time from outside my own congregation had ramped up so much that I had to devise a plan to make it all work without losing my mind or disappointing the people in my life. Here was the plan:

1. Hire an assistant to deal with all my public communications and details for speaking events.
2. Make coffee dates and pastoral care appointments for right up to the time I leave and right away after returning.
3. Eat real food.
4. Get real sleep.
5. Get real exercise.

My brilliant five-point plan for making it all work, for being it all (wife, mother, pastor, friend, writer, speaker), worked. Kind of.

Okay—it didn't work at all. I felt like a waiter balancing a too-high stack of plates—if I just kept moving and maneuvering, none of them would fall. It was important to me that nothing got dropped, and if the occasional need for sleeping pills and Netflix-and-chocolate-induced catatonic states was the price I paid, so be it.

That was the problem. On the outside, my plan looked like "good self-care," but really, it was just a laundry list of habits I adopted to ensure I could continue to overfunction. Maybe if white wine and cocaine would've given me the same results, I would have gone that route. As it was, I decided on CrossFit and an 8:30 bedtime.

But this strategy manifested itself as pure anxiety in my body. Not the kind where you forget how to walk or take air into your lungs—the ongoing, low-grade kind where you are always afraid, afraid of nothing in particular, and you feel as if your heartbeats have been replaced with the dun-dun, dun-dun music in horror films.

Each month I'd take the glass of water offered by Jane, sit in the armchair beside the window in her office, and say how scared I was of disappointing my parishioners. I was sure that all the plates were just about to fall and everyone I cared about would get nasty cuts on the bottom of their feet and they'd blame me. I was always just moments away from everyone resenting me. But if I could outrun the bad horror film soundtrack, keep moving, keep overfunctioning, then no one would think I'm the horrible person I've spent six years trying to convince lovely Jane that I am.

✦

By the time my parishioners Jeff and Tracy got engaged, my calendar had gotten so notoriously full that the first thing Jeff and Tracy did the following day wasn't to start finding a venue or post the news on Facebook—it was to call me and get their fall wedding, whose date was a year and a half in the future, on what they teasingly called their "celebrity pastor's calendar." I checked my calendar, which was clear, and I marked down their wedding date.

Tracy was just about to finish her doctorate in physical therapy, a degree she started when she moved to Denver three years earlier, which was also the time she'd started coming to House for All. She'd moved from Seattle, where she attended a sister church of ours—Church of the Apostles—and she knew when she moved that she would have a home with us. She's about the loudest person at church.[13] You never have to guess what Tracy is thinking. She has a beautiful faith and once told me that physical therapy is her Christian vocation; she serves God by helping people move their bodies.

Jeff is as quiet as you'd imagine an engineer who makes mirrors would be. Mirrors for outer space, no less. I guess things have to bounce off satellites somehow so, yeah—mirrors, for space. Jeff has a gorgeous bass voice, and he and Tracy are two of the very few actual ELCA Lutherans at our church. They met at House for All and fell in love there. And now they were going to be married.

Six months later, I was reviewing my speaking calendar when I saw something that didn't look right.

I texted Tracy: "Tracy, don't freak out. But what is the date of the wedding again?"

She texted back: "September 13. Why?"

September 13. FUCK. September 13 happened to be in the very middle of a two-week speaking tour in Australia that I had booked two weeks after agreeing to do Jeff and Tracy's wedding. Apparently

---

13. Which is saying a lot, since Rick Strandloff also goes to House for All.

my calendar had not been synching up with my assistant Lisa's calendar, so the wedding didn't show up when I agreed to the Australia trip.

Jeff and Tracy had every reason to expect the pastor who loves them to be the one to do their wedding. They'd planned *eighteen months* in advance to ensure she would be the one to stand before them as they took vows to spend their lives loving each other for better or worse. She had told them that they, and the other people at House for All Sinners and Saints, were a priority to her, and yet here she was, saying, "Oh gosh, my bad . . . I'll actually be gallivanting around Australia with a bunch of marsupials."

I e-mailed the Australia people, saying it was still a year off and if they could please shift the dates by a week, I would forgo my speaking fee. I felt the plates I'd been balancing shift. They replied. No. They had already spent ten thousand dollars renting a space and printing materials.

Tracy and Jeff then spent a couple of days trying to see if it was possible to change their date. I told them that if it cost more money I would give them the speaking fee I would get in Australia. But it wasn't possible. Jeff and Tracy had too many family members who had already arranged their lives around that date. Now my arms were shaking. I scrambled. Hey, Australia people, what if I personally asked Rachel Held Evans to do this gig instead of me?

No. They wanted me. Women are not ordained in the Lutheran church in Australia and they were at a point of needing to hear a strong female pastoral voice.

There was no amount of strength and movement that could prevent what was happening. It was a mess. I couldn't bring myself to say to Jeff and Tracy, "I am breaking my commitment to you so I can go to

Australia." And I also couldn't bring myself to say to the Australia folks, "Sorry about that ten-thousand-dollar thing, but I'm not coming."

There was no way I would come out of this looking good and, much more importantly, without harming someone in the process.

It's my practice to welcome new people to the church by making sure they know that House for All Sinners and Saints will, at some point, let them down. That I will say or do something stupid and disappoint them. And then I encourage them to decide *before* that happens if they will stick around *after* it happens. If they leave, I tell them, they will miss the way that God's grace comes in and fills in the cracks left behind by our brokenness. And that's too beautiful to miss.

"This is that time, isn't it?" Tracy asked in a text.

"Huh?" I replied.

"When you do or say something stupid and disappoint us."

"Damn it. Yeah. I think so."

I was dying. I hadn't remembered that. I mean, I had said it so many times, but the truth is that I would still rather be good than make a mistake and receive grace.

The next morning I awoke to an e-mail from Tracy.

Dear Pastor Nadia,

Jeff and I release you from the commitment to do our wedding. As much as this is painful, we understand why our pastor needs to be in Australia. We love you. And we forgive you.

We love you. And we forgive you.

So many tears.

I cried because I needed to be set free. I needed someone to say,

"Nadia, let the fucking plates drop," because fear of dropping them was torturing me and was, in the end, way worse than having them drop. And I cried because I had been so afraid for so long that my parishioners would start to feel ignored and would resent me, and I exhausted myself trying to prevent that, because I love them, and in the end, the thing I feared happened anyway, and I was okay and they were okay.

Later, as I sat and told Jane this story, one of many stories of grace shared over the course of the years, she said, "You've preached it for so long, yet were so afraid to have to need it."

She was right. It was as if all those sermons I'd preached had slowly built Jeff and Tracy into a grace silo for their own preacher. In the moment, when what I needed was love and grace and forgiveness, when I needed what I try to preach to others, they had enough to share, even though I had disappointed them.

And the thing about grace, real grace, is that it stings. It stings because if it's real it means we don't "deserve" it. No amount of my own movement or strength could have held up those plates I'd stacked way too high. I tried, and I failed, and Jeff and Tracy suffered for it, and then they extended to me kindness, compassion, and forgiveness out of their silo of hurt and grace.

Church is messed up. I know that. People, including me, have been hurt by it. But as my United Church of Christ pastor friend Heather says, "Church isn't perfect. It's practice." Among God's people, those who have been knocked on their asses by the grace of God, we practice giving and receiving the undeserved.

And receiving grace is basically the best shitty feeling in the world. I don't want to need it. Preferably I could just do it all and be it all and never mess up. That may be what I would prefer, but it is never what I need. I *need* to be broken apart and put back into a different shape by that merging of things human and divine, which is really screwing up and receiving grace and love and forgiveness rather than receiving what I really deserve. I need the very thing that I will do everything I can to avoid needing.

The sting of grace is not unlike the sting of being loved well, because when we are loved well, it is inextricably linked to all the times we have *not* been loved well, all the times we ourselves have not loved others well, and all the things we've done or not done that feel like evidence against our worthiness. Love and grace are such deceivingly soft words—but they both sting like hell and then go and change the shape of our hearts and make us into something we couldn't create ourselves to be.

✦

A year after Jeff and Tracy forgave me, I was in Sydney, Australia, standing in front of several hundred women at a private Christian school giving a talk about what I think the gospel is, when I went off my notes.

"Honestly, sometimes the gospel is just other people. Sometimes the only way God gets through to us is through God's agents, and two of those trained operatives are getting married today. Their names are Jeff and Tracy, and I want to tell you about them."

I told the whole story. And then I made them all promise to pray for them and their life together. I did. I actually made hundreds of Australian women pray right then and there for two people on the other side of the globe. Not because I felt guilty, but because I felt grateful.

19

--- ✦ ---

Blessed Are They

I t didn't matter that no one made the saint cookies this year. Not really. Our made-up pseudo tradition went the "you had to have been there" way of most inside jokes, as well it should have.

I hadn't even realized that the cookies were missing until I arrived at church that afternoon, on a clear, unusually warm first Sunday in November. Walking into our parish hall and seeing Amy Clifford unload stacks of white cloth and several boxes of candles onto the stage, I simultaneously remembered two things I had forgotten. It seems to happen that way, the things I have forgotten all making themselves known at once. As though my car keys, returning that phone call, my father's birthday, and the name of my hairdresser are all hanging out in the same dark corner of my mind smoking cigarettes and telling each other jokes, until they all decide it's time to show up.

When I got to the church that afternoon, two thoughts ran through my head—"I forgot about the saint cookies" and "I left the *New York Times* on the bench at Chipotle." I didn't care about the cookies. But the newspaper was for a small shrine I'd made for Suzanne Lynch for this year's feast of All Saints.

Rick Strandloff arrived moments later with a shrine he'd made for his own friend.[14] He saw me at one of the candle-covered tables setting up a picture of Suzanne—a lovely black-and-white portrait from when she was a fresh-faced lawyer in the 1970s, so young and filled with fierce intelligence. Rick had remembered reading her eulogy a few months earlier on my blog.

"That's her?" he asked.

I smoothed the white tablecloth into a more reliably flat surface onto which I could place a coffee cup and told him how, when I lived in her guest room, Suzanne and I had read the *New York Times* (she the news, I the entertainment section) every morning while we drank coffee, and that I had left the copy of the *Times* I had purchased to accompany her picture and this coffee cup at the Chipotle where I ate lunch, and that there was no time for me to get a replacement.

Fifteen minutes later, I felt a tap on my shoulder. Rick handed me a fresh copy of the Sunday *New York Times*. He spent six dollars of his very limited income on it.

"You need to have this," he said, with his manic blend of sincerity and enthusiasm. "It's important."

These small acts of love come so naturally to Rick. I've consistently witnessed this man love people with ease and extend kindness to everyone he encounters without ever a hint of judgment. When asked recently why I haven't "moved on" from House for All Sinners and Saints, all I could say was, "Because they keep changing me. I bump up against these people in holy, frustrating, and unimagined ways and realize at some point afterward that the shape of my heart has changed for the better."

---

14. I describe Rick, a con artist/ex-convict/amazing party planner with the heart of a servant, more fully in *Pastrix*. He's a manic and wonderful member of our community. And, most of the time, he's *very* loud.

More people arrived to set up photos and physical items to honor those who had died. There is a particular care that one takes with placing such ordinary, holy things on a table for display. There is a slowness to it, a frame-by-frame-ness to the action of placing a photo of your father and his old baseball glove down on a white table lined with candles—especially when just six months earlier you still could hold the hand that once used that glove. There is an intention to such a simple thing as laying a baseball glove or a *New York Times* on an All Saints' table.

As the tables filled with the names, pictures, and possessions of our beloved departed, and cards to accompany them, certain names stood out, as Alma White's had just five years earlier, but for different reasons. A card next to a flower, "miscarried child." A card, "M. M., killed by a drunk driver." Bobbie Jo's printout of the eulogy for her soul friend, Amy Mack, with a white rose next to the picture of Amy's empty wheel-chair in a mountain field.

It was standing room only at church that Sunday, and I didn't real-ize that Billy's mom was there until I caught her eye during the passing of the peace and placed my hand over my heart. When I could get near her, I realized she was holding a photo of Billy.

"The thing you said about how if loving Billy was enough to keep him alive, he would still be here? That was what I really needed some-one to say that day," she told me, eyes welling. We hugged, then she gently pushed me away as though to say, "I'm okay, go hug some other folks now."

I hadn't known she was in the room earlier when I had preached, even mentioning her in the sermon. I had preached that it can be easy to view the Beatitudes—the "blessed ares" that had just been read—as Jesus's command for us to try real hard to be meeker, poorer, and mourn-ier in order that we might be blessed in the eyes of God.

And since the Beatitudes are always the gospel reading for All Saints' Sunday, it can make the people who are called saints seem so unattainably good and the people who aren't (that would be us) feel unworthy. Plus, it can be easy to look at, say, Mother Teresa and think, *Well, she is a saint because she was meek. So if I, too, want to be blessed, I should try to be meek like her.* (Don't get me wrong, we could use a few more people trying to be like Mother Teresa. I just don't think that her virtue of meekness is what made her considered blessed by Jesus.)

But what if the Beatitudes aren't about a list of conditions we should try to meet to be blessed? What if they are not virtues we should aspire to? What if Jesus saying "blessed are the meek" is not instructive but performative—that the pronouncement of blessing is actually what confers the blessing itself? Maybe the Sermon on the Mount is all about Jesus's lavish blessing of the people around him on that hillside, blessing all the accidental saints in this world, especially those who that world—like ours—didn't seem to have much time for: people in pain, people who work for peace instead of profit, people who exercise mercy instead of vengeance.

Maybe Jesus was simply blessing the ones around him that day who didn't otherwise receive blessing, who had come to believe that, for them, blessings would never be in the cards. I mean, come on, doesn't that just *sound* like something Jesus would do? Extravagantly throwing around blessings as though they grew on trees?

So on that All Saints' Sunday, I imagined Jesus standing among us offering some new beatitudes, and I said to the congregation:

Blessed are the agnostics.

Blessed are they who doubt. Those who aren't sure, who can still be surprised.

Blessed are they who are spiritually impoverished and therefore not so certain about everything that they no longer take in new information.

Blessed are those who have nothing to offer.

Blessed are the preschoolers who cut in line at communion.

Blessed are the poor in spirit.

You are of heaven and Jesus blesses you.

Blessed are they for whom death is not an abstraction.

Blessed are they who have buried their loved ones, for whom tears could fill an ocean. Blessed are they who have loved enough to know what loss feels like.

Blessed are the mothers of the miscarried.

Blessed are they who don't have the luxury of taking things for granted anymore.

Blessed are they who can't fall apart because they have to keep it together for everyone else. Blessed are the motherless, the alone, the ones from whom so much has been taken. Blessed are those who "still aren't over it yet."

Blessed are Larry's wife and Billy's mom and Amy Mack's friends.

Blessed are those who mourn.

You are of heaven and Jesus blesses you.

Blessed are those who no one else notices. The kids who sit alone at middle-school lunch tables. The laundry guys at the hospital. The sex workers and the night-shift street sweepers.

Blessed are the losers and the babies and the parts of ourselves that are so small, the parts of ourselves that don't want to make eye contact with a world that loves only the winners.

Blessed are the forgotten.

Blessed are the closeted.

Blessed are the unemployed, the unimpressive, the underrepresented.

Blessed are the teens who have to figure out ways to hide the new cuts on their arms. Blessed are the meek.

You are of heaven and Jesus blesses you.

Blessed are the wrongly accused, the ones who never catch a break, the ones for whom life is hard, for Jesus chose to surround himself with people like them.

Blessed are those without documentation.

Blessed are the ones without lobbyists.

Blessed are foster kids and trophy kids and special ed kids and every other kid who just wants to feel safe and loved.

Blessed are those who hunger and thirst for righteousness.

Blessed are they who know there has to be more than this. Because they are right.

Blessed are those who make terrible business decisions for the sake of people.

Blessed are the burned-out social workers and the overworked teachers and the pro bono case takers.

Blessed are the kindhearted NFL players and the fundraising trophy wives.

Blessed are the kids who step between the bullies and the weak.

Blessed are they who hear that they are forgiven.

Blessed is everyone who has ever forgiven me when I didn't deserve it.

Blessed are the merciful, for they totally get it.

I imagined Jesus standing there blessing us all because I believe that is our Lord's nature. Because, after all, it was Jesus who had all the powers of the universe at his disposal but did not consider his equality with God something to be exploited. Instead, he came to us in the most vulnerable of ways, as a powerless, flesh-and-blood newborn. As if to say, "You may hate your bodies, but I am blessing all human flesh. You may admire strength and might, but I am blessing all human weakness. You may seek power, but I am blessing all human vulnerability." This Jesus whom we follow cried at the tomb of his friend and turned the other cheek and forgave those who hung him on a cross. He *was* God's Beatitude—God's blessing to the weak in a world that admires only the strong.

Later, as we cleaned up after liturgy, stacking chairs, breaking down tables, blowing out candles, I picked up the tall, black-flecked paschal candle. My hand felt the smooth wax, poured seven months earlier by Victoria, and noted that while the impurities of the burned-down remains of the previous year's candles were visible deep in the wax, the sides were smooth and pure white. I thought, *What is this coming together to live and tell and be made into the story of Jesus if not a melting and being re-formed?*

We expose ourselves to the brightness of God's light and it warms us for a while, but eventually we melt. Our resistances and plans and schemes and scars and pride all melt down in times when we are forgiven by friends, and when Jesus tags unflattering photos of us, and when we embrace the thing we were trying to hide from (in others and ourselves), and when we meet someone else's need, and when we take the Eucharist to a dying woman (who saved our sorry twenty-three-year-old ass).

When all of it is given meaning in the larger story of Jesus Christ, it destroys us, then pours our melted selves back into another form that still bears the marks of how we got there.

Then we become something that can bear light, the brightness of which is not diminished, even when divided and borrowed.

And we pray, O God, rule, govern, and preserve with your continual protection your whole church, giving us peace in this time of our paschal rejoicing; through the same Lord Jesus Christ, your Son, who lives and reigns with you and the Holy Spirit, one God, now and forever. Amen.

A Note to Readers

The stories in this book are told to the best of my memory. Some identifying details have been changed to protect the privacy of some really amazing people. In places, I've condensed time lines for the sake of narrative flow. As with any memoir, the story I recall and tell may differ in some respects from how others would have experienced the same event.

Most of these stories center around the practices and people of my congregation, House for All Sinners and Saints. For their sake, I ask that if, after reading this book you are intrigued and want to know or experience more, consider engaging with us online. We need to reserve our very limited physical space at liturgy for those in the Denver area who are searching for a community. Thank you for understanding.

Having said that, if you want a community like the one you've just read about, I bet you are not the only one in your town who feels this way. So do what we did: Gather a small number of people once a month to simply share a meal and pray together. Talk about your lives and what is happening in the world. Be yourselves. Extend grace. Read the gospel . . . and repeat. (Since ancient times, saints and sinners have called this mysteriously transformative experience "church.") See for yourself what happens. You might be surprised. I sure was.

Acknowledgments

I have many more supportive and loving people in my life than I likely deserve and without whom I could not possibly do what I do.

My gratitude goes to:

My church, which is so generous with sharing me.

My family, who is so generous in loving me.

My editors—Nicci, who is infuriating but totally knows how to get my best out of me, and Dave, who never seemed flustered by my BS.

My agent, Greg, who has my back.

Friends and fellow writers who gave me amazing feedback on this project: Barbara Lehr, Sara Miles, Domenica Ruta, Phil Harrison, and Heather Kopp.

The people who made me countless cups of coffee at Hooked on Colfax.

The people at CFPH who don't give a shit about anything I do outside of our gym.

And Zacchaeus, the Greatest of Great Danes.

Thank you.

Discussion Questions

1. In the first chapter, Nadia writes, "*All* the saints I've known have been accidental ones—people who inadvertently stumbled into redemption. . . . What makes us the saints of God is not our ability to be saintly but rather God's ability to work through sinners." Is there anyone in your own life whom you would consider a "saint" or perhaps an *accidental* saint? Why? Do you ever think of yourself as a saint?

2. Nadia writes, "I stumble into holy moments not realizing where I am until they are over. I love poorly, then accidentally say the right thing at the right moment without even realizing it . . . show tenderness when it's needed, and then turn around and think of myself way too often." Do you find yourself caught in a similar kind of conflict? What do such experiences reveal to you about our attempts to be "good"? about God? about yourself?

3. Nadia says that, at the cross, "Jesus takes our crap and exchanges it for his blessedness." Have you seen this exchange take place in your life? in another's? What blessedness have you received in return for "crap"? What was the result?

4. In chapter 4, Nadia writes that if she were Jonah, speaking at youth events would be her Nineveh. But, "sometimes the fact

that there is nothing about you that makes you the right person to do something is exactly what God is looking for." What is your "Nineveh"? Has God ever moved you to confront that thing, person, or event that you would rather avoid? What happened, and how did it feel?

5. Nadia describes how "selfless" acts can still inspire a covert kind of pride that's difficult to resist. Have you ever felt like you were someone's "project"—as if they were trying to "minister" to you, yet somehow were serving themselves? How did it feel? Why is it so difficult for us to give to others without becoming self-important?

6. When you were young, did you believe, like Nadia, that *godliness* meant following a list of prohibitions: no swearing, no lying, no listening to rock music, no sexual yearning, no drinking alcohol, and no snarky back talk? Has that rules-based messaging affected how you live and feel as an adult? Is there such a thing as "godly living"? Is the lifestyle and personality of the Christian the primary focus of faith?

7. Nadia writes about the Annunciation, the moment in the Gospels when the angel tells Mary that God will supernaturally give her a son. "If I had been in her place, which would be harder for me to believe? The part about being knocked up by God and giving birth to a king? Or the part where the angel said I was favored?" Do you struggle to believe that God favors you? Why? What does it even mean to "have God's favor"?

8. After the Sandy Hook school shooting in December 2012, Nadia writes, "We were left wondering, 'Where the hell is God?'" When have you asked this question? What conclusion did you reach? What would you tell someone who asks you this question?

9. Do you agree or disagree when Nadia writes that Christianity often becomes sentimental in a way that fails to acknowledge (and minister to) "a world where we see up-to-the-minute images of human suffering"? What does it look like to embrace the hope of the gospel without becoming escapist?

10. When Nadia was too angry to lead her congregants one evening, she found comfort and healing in a friend's prayer and in holding another friend's baby, "because sometimes only beauty can release ugliness." What "beautiful" things have smoothed life's ugliness for you? When you feel too beaten down to carry on, what strengthens you? What beautiful thing can you offer to others in ugly places?

11. After confronting her fear of mountain driving on the road near Jericho, Nadia describes the experience as "a spiritual exfoliation by humiliation" and writes, "My heart was now available." Do you identify with Nadia's want for independence? Has a humbling experience ever scraped that independence away and left you softer toward others? How can we learn to welcome rather than avoid our own neediness?

12. How does it feel to know Jesus "spent his time with people for whom life was not easy"? Do you ever judge yourself when your

life becomes hard? Have you ever felt like the outsider, who wasn't easily understood or welcomed by a group of people, even the church?

13. Nadia writes, "Whenever people annoy me beyond reason, I can guarantee it's because they're demonstrating something I'd rather not see in myself." Do you find this to be true in your own life? Describe some people who annoy you. What traits do they exhibit, and do you recognize any of them in yourself? How can we change our attitudes toward such people?

14. Reflecting on Maundy Thursday, Nadia writes, "In the end, we aren't punished *for* our sins as much as we are punished *by* our sins." Have you ever felt punished *by* a sin of your own? Why is it so hard for us to receive forgiveness, even when we feel the toxic effects that sin can cause in us?

15. When Nadia's Unitarian friend Andie says, "I think I'm having a crisis of faith . . . I think I believe in Jesus," Nadia responds, "I'm so sorry, but sometimes Jesus just hunts your ass down and there's nothing you can do about it." Have you ever felt "hunted down" by Jesus? How did it feel? Does it encourage you to hear that five years after her "crisis" Andie was leading the Easter liturgy at House for All?

16. "In a way, all our alleluias are a little tacky and/or a little moldy." What do you hear Nadia suggesting by this statement? What can you do with your own messed-up alleluias?

17. "God's mercy is . . . a blunt instrument," Nadia writes, "the kind that kills the thing that wronged it and resurrects something new in its place." Have you ever experienced mercy as an agent of painful yet redemptive change? What died, and what was "resurrected" as a result? How would you describe God's forgiving passion for his people?

18. Nadia writes that "the beautiful, radical grace that flows from the heart of God to God's broken and blessed humanity" is impossible to find outside of community. How does that statement make you feel? Do you recognize ways in which you try to manufacture God's grace on your own? How do we balance the need for community with the equal importance of carving out times of solitude?

19. Nadia believes it is "our Lord's nature" to bless us. Do you ever find that difficult to believe in your own life? What does it mean to be blessed by God? And how does it change us?

20. "God wants you, you in your imperfect, broken, shimmering glory." Do you identify with this statement? What does it mean to be imperfect and broken, yet shimmering and somehow glorious? Why do you think it's in this state that God wants us?

A Conversation with the Author

⁘

We wanted to invite Nadia to share more with her readers on her process and motivations for writing *Accidental Saints*. For this interview, David Kopp and Derek Reed, editors at Convergent Books, posed the questions.

You're a busy pastor. What kept you at your keyboard when you were writing *Accidental Saints*?

I guess I think we're in a time in the life of the church where stories of failure are so much more important than stories of success. And I just have so much of that kind of material to work with, so I kept writing!

For so long, Christians have told hagiographies of the saints and held those stories up as the ideal that we should strive toward. And yet, today, those stories are received with skepticism.

Right. Unless human nature itself has somehow changed in a dramatic way, then I think that God's work in the world is and has always been done through sinners. There's nothing wrong with that. Sometimes the people least qualified are the ones God's looking for, and I think that's a more inspiring message than, "Here's this example of gleaming piety that you should try to emulate."

You're very open about your personal story, and in some of the stories you tell—if not most of them—you take a lot of risks.

Was there a story in *Accidental Saints* that was most difficult for you to tell?

The story about Amy and Bobbie. That was the hardest, most vulnerable one, because I had to admit something I've spent my entire life trying to avoid. But it ended up being my favorite story in the book. I've spent my entire life trying to avoid vulnerability. My M.O. was to appear as strong as possible so that no one would ever take advantage of me. I thought that no one could hurt me if I was powerful and strong all the time. But the irony is that I'm actually at my most powerful when I'm vulnerable.

I think my congregation taught me that, in a sense. When I first started House for All, I met a woman who's now one of my best friends, Sara Miles, and I was lamenting to her that I didn't have a pastor's personality. I was like, "What am I going to do?" And she said, "Honey, don't worry. Your people will make you into the pastor they need you to be." I think that has absolutely come true. My congregation needs me to be the kind of pastor who's deeply confessional in my preaching, who's willing to be vulnerable. They needed that from me, so that's who I've become.

Talk about your CrossFit obsession. Is there a spiritual dimension to that? Or is that angry, isolationist Nadia recovering from your life as a pastor?

I like to say that CrossFit helps me leave some of the more inelegant aspects of my personality in the form of sweat on the gym floor every morning. It's like *exor*-cise, you know?

It's also my social scene—those are the people I hang out with in my spare time. I love that I have a space in my life that is so separate, in a way, from everything else, and I get to be known and wanted in one space in my life that has nothing to do with what I do in the world. Is it "spiritual"? I don't really think of it as such, no.

But surely the people at your gym have questions about your work as a pastor, right?

They all know what I do; they just don't care. To tell you the truth, almost all of my social life is spent with people who aren't churchgoers. I think that's healthy. I think pastors should have a space in which they're liked and known apart from what they do.

At CrossFit, you practice hard. You have a coach, you're working at your strength and conditioning, and so on. But in *Accidental Saints*, when you're writing about the spiritual life, you say, "Good luck with trying to improve yourself. You can't get there from here; you can't try hard enough. You're not improvable." Talk about that contrast.

There are things you can do to improve your physical body—you can eat better, you can exercise more, you can lift weights. But I don't think we can improve our spiritual selves by exerting effort. At least I haven't experienced it. For some people, maybe their spiritual self is improved through practices. But for me, any shift I've experienced on a spiritual level has almost always happened despite myself, not because of myself.

As Americans, we're big believers in self improvement. We believe that if you just work hard and apply yourself, you can improve, and I think we've imported that into our lives as Christians in a way that can be really harmful.

Is there something about the ancient traditions of the church—the sacraments, the liturgies, the candles, the chants—that's modern? It seems like there's something about it that works, not just in your church but increasingly among Millennials.

Many of the people in my congregation have a lot of chaos in their lives. It could be because they're counselors for people who just experienced sexual assault, or they're working with homeless or pregnant teenagers. Or it could be because they're holding it together with transparent tape in their personal lives—they have mental health issues, they're dealing with instability or addiction, or with trying to integrate their identity for the first time. So, having a deeply liturgical and sacramental space in that chaos, a space where they can come and hear the same words each week, it provides a kind of stability to their life.

Like, the Kyrie has been around for what, a couple millennia? For generations, the faithful have said, "Lord have mercy, Christ have mercy, Lord have mercy," and there's a way in which just adding your voice to that chorus can root you in the midst of the chaos in your life. The liturgy has its own integrity to it—it doesn't demand my integrity in order to be efficacious. We get to enter this thing that stands on its own and doesn't demand a particular type of piety or emotional feeling or even *belief* from us. We're just adding our voices to the prayers of the faithful, and it slowly forms who we are. That's why I like to say that we have to be deeply rooted in tradition in order to innovate with integrity.

It doesn't require belief to work?

No, it doesn't. I'm surprisingly unconcerned with what people in my church believe. Belief is going to be influenced by all sorts of things that I have nothing to do with, so I don't feel responsible for that. I'm responsible for what they *hear*—and hearing the gospel, the good news about who God is, slowly forms us over time. I don't find belief (intellectually assenting to a set of theological propositions) to be the core of Christianity in the way a lot of people do.

Many people are moving away from traditional church for the reason you're describing here — that the church's emphasis on belief doesn't work for them. You feel similarly about the emphasis on belief, but you've moved *further* into religion. Comment on that.

When I say I'm religious, it has to do less with belief than with what I'm exposed to on a regular basis, what my symbol system is, what my practice is in terms of being a Christian in a community — these are what end up forming belief — like I believe in grace because I've experienced grace through the story of Jesus and the receiving of the Eucharist and the messiness of being in a community of other Christians. Take the Good Friday liturgy, for example. The fact that we have access to this story of who God is in the presence of suffering allows us to have a reference point for when suffering happens in our lives. We get this frame or container — these stories, liturgies, and practices — which help us to know how to hold the tragedy, violence, and suffering we experience in the world and in our lives. If we didn't have that framework, it would just feel so free floating. Religion at its best allows us a kind of rootedness that I find meaningful.

What do you say to someone who comes to House for All and says that he or she admires the story and example of Jesus but aren't inclined to self-identify as a Christian?

My friend Sara says that the really inconvenient thing about being Christian is the fact that God is revealed in other people, and other

208 ✛ A Conversation with the Author

people are annoying. I understand the impulse of not wanting to be in community. I can't argue with that. But I think the experience of bumping up against other people has changed me in ways that I never could have been changed if I was just reading books and practicing meditation. We don't get to be Christians on our own. It's really inconvenient, and I wish there were a different setup for that. But that's what we were handed.

John Cheever said his stories always started because he felt an intensity of feeling about a person or an incident or a scene. You're not a novelist, but I think you do write in much of the same way. So much of this book started, not as an idea, but as an intensely felt story in your life.

My belief and my faith, all come from experience. All of it. I would stop writing these stories if they would just stop happening to me!

I'm not a Christian apologist—I'm not trying to convince anybody of anything. All I'm doing is saying, "This is what I believe to be true, because this is my experience, and here's the belief that this experience illuminates." The weird thing is that I'm also a pretty orthodox Lutheran theologian at the same time.

How did you get through seminary, when your faith is based so much more on experience than on belief?

I don't care much about ideas, unless those ideas are helping you to stumble upon the meaning in real events, real things, bodies, and people. If there's an idea that helps you understand the meaning behind actual stuff, then it's great. If it doesn't, I don't give a shit about it. But that's the thing about the gospel. More than anything else out there, the gospel helps us pull ideas into the dirt of experience in a way that puts meaning behind what happens in our lives.

Talk about the meaning of the Eucharist in light of what you've said about experience vs. belief, and participating in something physical as a door to God.

That's the crazy thing about Christianity—the idea that the finite can contain the infinite. After all, what is the incarnation if not that? So there's an incredible physicality to the spiritual within the Christian story. There's not this weird sort of Greek separation, where there's a higher spiritual world and a corrupted, bad world of flesh. It's all one. Because if God chose to have a body, there's a way in which spiritual things are revealed in the physical things that are all around us—bread, wine, people, tears, laughter.

Do you see your writing as an act of inviting people into a sacrament, in the same way that you do when you're standing in front of the church?

Writing isn't sacramental per se, but I do hope that it points to something bigger than me. If people read something that I write, and their reaction is about me instead of reacting about themselves and God, then I don't think I've succeeded. If the reaction is, "Nadia and her church are cool," that's hardly worth writing about. But if, somehow, my telling of these stories invites people into a space where they can consider something true and broken and beautiful about themselves—or if it drives them to seek community in which bread is broken and shared, and they are told it's the body of Christ and it's for forgiveness and it's for them—if that's the response, then it's totally worth it. It's not about me or my particular congregation. It's about this invitation we all have to the life of God.

Is there a particular kind of person who you hope *doesn't* pick up the book?

Not really. That's what surprised me about my last book. There were people who liked it who I was sure would hate it.

What is it about your message that energizes those unlikely people?

I'd say, Christian freedom. I'm not bound by legalism and shame. I'm free in who I am, and my congregation is free to live as Christians in a way that makes sense for us. People don't talk enough about what the freedom of a Christian looks like. We focus on what the law looks like, what morality looks like, what the Christian lifestyle looks like, but we never talk about the *freedom* of a Christian. It's a profound, beautiful, hilarious freedom that I think draws people to it in a way that focus on "the lifestyle of a Christian" doesn't.

A lot of people don't experience that kind of freedom, and they're hungry for it. Yet instead, people have been fed spoonfuls of nonsense and told it was Jesus.

You write about "the sting of grace." What do you mean by that?

There's this power of God in the universe that is restorative and redemptive, and no one is worthy of it, but everyone gets to receive it. It's powerful, but it's offensive at the same time, because it's not fair, and it doesn't work into our notions of justice. It changes us, and it's what we need, but it doesn't mean it feels good. If it's real grace, it's never going to feel good.

A Conversation with the Author ✦ 211

Richard Rohr says that the people who've truly experienced grace—meaning they're not worthy of it and they still get it—are no longer in a position of being able to decide who "the deserving poor" are. When you realize that no one's worthy and yet everyone receives (the practice of the church that illuminates this idea is the open table at the Eucharist), where's the moral high ground that you stand on anymore? The only ground you get to stand on is the ground at the foot of the cross, with all the rest of us sinners. But it's holy ground. It's a position of standing in and among, and in solidarity with everyone, and singing praise to God. It's a very different way of seeing Christianity, I think.

Your book is intentionally not prescriptive, but is there something you want to happen with your readers once they put down the book?

I want them to begin to see how real grace and mercy and forgiveness and brokenness and beauty are around them, in their lives. I guarantee the things that happen to me are happening to them, too. I just happen to think about this stuff so obsessively that it ends up feeling like having a not-very-interesting mental illness. But the glory of God in the midst of our crap is revealed all the time, all around us. What I hope is that people would read the book and see that and realize how transformative it can be.